The IEA Health and Welfare Unit

Choice in Welfare No. 18

Rising Crime and the Dismembered Family

Dedicated to

John Maxwell Norman Dennis
Born 10 September 1993
In Pensacola

The IEA Health and Welfare Unit

Choice in Welfare No. 18

Rising Crime and the Dismembered Family

How Conformist Intellectuals Have Campaigned Against Common Sense

Norman Dennis

IEA Health and Welfare Unit
London, 1993

First published in October 1993
by
The IEA Health and Welfare Unit
2 Lord North St
London SW1P 3LB

© The IEA Health and Welfare Unit 1993

ISBN 0-255 36350-8

Typeset by the IEA Health and Welfare Unit
in Palatino 11 on 12 point
Printed in Great Britain by
Goron Pro-Print Co. Ltd
Churchill Industrial Estate, Lancing, West Sussex

Contents

Foreword

In *Rising Crime and the Dismembered Family* Norman Dennis develops further the argument first advanced in his and George Erdos' seminal study, *Families Without Fatherhood*. He calls attention to the role of a new class of 'conformist intellectuals' in undermining what common sense tells us about rising crime and family breakdown. Usually armed with a self-image of anti-establishment radicalism, conformist intellectuals deny that the family is breaking down. It has, they say, only been changing. Nor, in the conformist's view, has there been a rise in crime, only an increase in 'moral panic'.

Norman Dennis demolishes these claims by carefully drawing attention to the unadorned facts, and he highlights a wider problem which has affected academic life on both sides of the Atlantic: that social affairs intellectuals are strongly inclined to subscribe to the politically-correct doctrines of the day. The result is that universities, instead of being havens for fearless seekers after truth, have become easy berths for conformists who are reluctant to allow the inconvenient facts to spoil a good theory.

Freedom of the Press Combats Political Correctness

Fortunately, the role of the academic as the bold investigator and iconoclastic commentator has been taken on by the press and it is due largely to the courage of some journalists that it has proved possible to stimulate a public debate about rising crime and family breakdown.

It was during 1989 that the IEA set out to draw attention to the growing problems caused by the decline of the traditional family. It embarked on a research programme linked to a series of 'consensus conferences' which were intended to bring together analysts of differing views to explore the extent and nature of their contrasting opinions. Financial support for the project initially came from the Dulverton Trust which supported the first consensus conference in February 1990. From April 1990, the Joseph Rowntree Foundation provided a major grant towards the project and particular praise should go to Richard Best for recommending support for a project greeted with more than a little scepticism by some of his colleagues. The main funding for the research work came from the Esmée Fairbairn Charitable Trust, and our special thanks go to Sir Robert Andrew and the Trustees.

Gaining support from trusts which see it as their task to support pioneering projects was not the most difficult problem. The real challenge was to break through the barrier of political correctness which had closed the minds of the great majority of academics. There were no more than a handful willing to face the wrath of their colleagues and Professor Halsey of the University of Oxford and Norman Dennis of the University of Newcastle upon Tyne deserve high praise for their courage in speaking out.

No less important in facilitating public debate was the freedom of the press. Among the first journalists to break the mould in the national press was Nick Wood with a report in *The Times* on 5 June 1990. He followed up with a piece in October of that year[1] and again in July 1991[2] with an article headed, 'Professor shudders for the next generation', which reported Professor Halsey's remarks, made at an IEA seminar, that many children brought up in one-parent families were not flourishing.

The next batch of reports followed some remarks by Peter Dawson, then secretary of the Professional Association of Teachers, who quoted Professor Halsey's comments as reported in Nick Wood's article. He became the target for angry criticism by single-mother lobbyists. Columnists then began to pick up the story. Heather Kirby was among the first to produce a serious column, also in *The Times*,[3] and on the same day Melanie Phillips wrote a hard-hitting piece for *The Guardian*.

Interest lapsed until the publication of *Families Without Fatherhood* in September 1992. It attracted serious attention from journalists, but academics generally preferred to give it the cold shoulder. Notable were articles by Suzanne Moore in *The Guardian*, Norman Macrae in *The Sunday Times* and Clifford Longley in *The Times*. More recently, Janet Daley of *The Times* has focused attention on the issue and Paul Barker has produced a thoughtful review in *The Times Literary Supplement*.[4] Norman Macrae, with characteristic fearlessness, has returned to the theme from time to time and *The Sunday Times* has generally provided space for regular careful discussion, focusing especially on the work of Charles Murray.

Melanie Phillips produced several columns in *The Guardian* and the *Observer* and more lately an article in *The Tablet*. Melanie Phillips perhaps deserves most praise for her courage in ramming home to readers of *The Guardian* and the *Observer* what must have been an unwelcome message.

In *The Tablet* she has put on record the attitude she found typical among social affairs intellectuals. Following the IEA seminar in July 1991 she had telephoned a prominent social scientist of the left to ask for details of the research findings on which he based his hostility to the claims of Halsey and Dennis that children from broken homes performed less well. It is worth reproducing her words in full:

> he released a stream of emotional invective, calling into question the mental faculties of those distinguished academics and asking excitedly: "What do these people want? Do they want unhappy parents to stay together?" After being pressed repeatedly to identify the research which repudiated the Halsey-Dennis thesis, he said, in summary, this: of course it was correct as far as the research was concerned, but where did that get anyone? Nowhere! Was it possible to turn back the clock? Of course not! And why were they so concerned above all else for the rights of the child? What about the rights of the parents, which were just as important?

The left's problem, according to Melanie Phillips, is that it has 'elevated the pursuit of individual gratification into a noble and heroic ideal'. No one lifestyle could be admitted to be better than any other for fear of offending minority sensibilities, so that, 'Gradually, no one was allowed to be normal. The very word was an affront'.[5]

This excessive individualism is not, however, confined to the left. And we all urgently need to accept responsibility to do our bit to refashion a new consensus on family life.

Fortunately, the intellectual conformists are now on the retreat. The freedom of the press and the courage of a few academics like Norman Dennis and Professor Halsey has saved us from monolithic political correctness. The next task is to discover what can be done to restore the ideal of the two-parent family, supported by the grandparents and aunts and uncles of the extended family, and in doing so to avoid resort to extremes, always a possibility when it becomes necessary to correct fundamentals. No one has done more than Norman Dennis to help reconstruct a new, moderate and attainable ideal of family life, and for this reason *Crime and the Dismembered Family* deserves the same careful attention that *Families Without Fatherhood* has received.

David G. Green

The Author

Norman Dennis was born in 1929 and spent his childhood in various working-class neighbourhoods during the depression years in Sunderland, County Durham, a sea-faring, ship-building and coal-mining town on the north-east coast of England. A crucially formative year was spent at the beginning of the Second World War living with a coal-miner's family in a small colliery village, Leasingthorne, County Durham. Admitted from Sunderland's grammar school to Corpus Christi College, Oxford, he preferred to study at the London School of Economics of Tawney, Popper, Ginsberg and Laski. He has been a Ford Fellow, Rockefeller Fellow, and Fellow of the Center for Advanced Study in the Behavioural Sciences at Palo Alto, California. He has carried out research into working-class communities from the Universities of Leeds, Bristol, Birmingham, Durham and Newcastle. Married with two children and two grandchildren, he is currently Reader in Social Studies at the University of Newcastle upon Tyne.

*Men are qualified for civil liberty
in exact proportion to their
disposition to put moral chains upon
their own appetites;*

*in proportion as their love of justice
is above their rapacity;*

*in proportion as their soundness and
sobriety of understanding
is above their vanity and presumption;*

*in proportion as they are more
disposed to listen to the counsels of
the wise and good,
in preference to the flattery of knaves.*

*Society cannot exist unless a
controlling power upon will and
appetite be placed somewhere,
and the less of it there is within,
the more there must be without.*

*It is ordained in the eternal
constitution of things
that men of intemperate minds
cannot be free.
Their passions forge their fetters.*

Burke
*Letter to a Member
of the National Assembly*

*The hungry sheep look up,
and are not fed,
But swolln with wind
and the rank mist they draw,
Rot inwardly,
and foul contagion spread;
Besides what the grim wolf
with privy paw
Daily devours apace, and nothing said.*

Milton
Lycidas

Preface

The argument in this essay comes from a life-time of conversation with my oldest friend, A.H. (Chelly) Halsey, who co-authored *English Ethical Socialism* with me. Our views on the role of intellectuals and especially contemporary pundits of social affairs are identical, and our explanation of both family change and its consequences are a straightforward inference from ethical socialism applied to the facts. We refuse to ignore the findings of research on the life chances of the child from the family where both parents were married when the child was born, and where both parents successfully struggled to stay together to look after it. The life chances of such a child are on the average better than those of the child from any other situation of conception and child-rearing that is at all possible on a large scale, and much better than those of the child from the father-absent situation. We want social policy and, of greater significance, the sound public opinion that must underpin it, to begin with the recognition of that truth.

Through the good offices of my old friend Dr. D.G. Green, and having survived the IEA's refereeing process, I am publishing this essay through the Institute of Economic Affairs, as a contribution to his efforts to explore the moral basis of a free society, consonant with the facts as far as we can honestly establish them, without which his ideal of civic capitalism is as much a chimera as my ideal of ethical socialism.

Professor Halsey intends to submit evidence to the Labour Party's Commission on Social Justice advocating support for the socialism that springs from strong families. Both his submission and my essay tell essentially the same story.

My largest debt of longest standing is to Chelly Halsey and next, 'in the precincts of battle', to David Green. But for many years some members of the Department of Social Policy at the University of Newcastle upon Tyne have met at lunch time on Thursdays, and have continued to meet when they have gone on to other (we would never admit better) places, as George Erdos has gone to the Department of Psychology, and Jon Davies has gone on to become Head of the Department of Religious Studies. The influence of the great authority on Durkheim, W.S.F. Pickering, still more than lingers in his absence at far-away Oxford. Friends who have retired often come back to join in the discussions about anything under the sun, Peter Collison, Betty Gittus and Harry Powell. David Robinson and Alan Hind, doing real work and pursuing left-wing causes, come as our former students to let us know what is really going on in the world.

Hardly ever absent and for that reason as for others the pillars of the group are Ahmed al Shahi, John Kennedy and of course George Erdos. It is thus a very mixed group: sociologists, including a sociologist of religion, anthropologists, a social psychologist and statisticians, one of whom is particularly interested in the philosophy of science. Always welcome are less regular attenders from other disciplines, including the disciplines of demography and social policy. Though the group is mixed in its final as well as its initial position on any particular topic, it would probably strike the outsider as predominantly liberal-left, but with the strongest single contingent explicitly labelling themselves 'ethical socialists'.

For several months George Erdos and I have been preoccupied together with the current version of the oldest problem of social philosophy and politics: what is the best attainable balance between the liberty of the individual and the common good and, under the specific conditions of contemporary British society, how can the desirable balance be struck a little more exactly? An aspect of that has been a discussion of the recent changes in the structures within which children are reared. An aspect of that in turn has been the recent role of intellectuals, by commission or omission, in helping bring them about. My focus is thus quite a narrow one. My intention is not to deal directly with the *causes* of the deterioration of civil life in this country and the *causes* of the changes in the institutions of kinship. I touch on these enormously important matters only in passing. I also only touch on the *relationship* between rising crime and the dismembered family. My primary concern here is with the failure of British society for the past thirty years or so to face up to the growing seriousness of its problems of citizenship and child-rearing.

The problems have not been faced because it has been systematically and successfully denied that there were any such problems. The growth in crime has been dismissed as the creation of ill-

informed people in the throes of a moral panic. The withdrawal of men from parenthood within a family setting has been celebrated as an improvement on the situation which had previously prevailed.

But there are, at last, many signs that the pernicious consensus shared by conformist social-affairs' intellectuals is crumbling under the sheer weight of the facts that contradict it. If this essay plays any part in hastening its collapse it will have served its purpose. The more conformists who come forward to deny they were ever part of such a consensus, and later (as is typically the case) to deny that such a consensus ever existed, the more hopeful the future will look.

Norman Dennis
Sunderland
10 September 1993

Acknowledgements

This essay originated as a lecture prepared for Family and Youth Concern on the occasion of its twenty-second annual meeting held on 26 June 1993, on the welcome instigation of Robert Whelan and Valerie Riches, who have worked longer and harder on this subject than I have.

1

Civic Safety and the Family Transformed

Thirty or forty years ago two features of everyday life in England began their extraordinary transformation, the results of which are now beyond all denial. One was in the prevalence of criminal conduct. The other was in the attitudes and activities associated with family life, as that term had been understood for at least the preceding one hundred years.

In 1955 crime was still recognizably at the level it had maintained since the middle of the nineteenth century, though it had recently broken the barrier of the 1,000 crimes per 100,000 of the population. The crime rate had been below 1,000 per 100,000 year by year and decade by decade. Through the blessings of peace-time and the stresses laid upon society by the absence and death of fathers at war; through boom and slump; through low unemployment and high unemployment; through the horrors of the mid-Victorian urban experience and the gradually emerging welfare state, for most of the period it had been stable at about half that level, rising gradually from just before the Great War to the early 1950s.

It then began its rapid rise. By 1960 the rate had risen by 700 per 100,000, to 1,700 per 100,000, that is, it had risen in the short period 1955-60 by more than the total annual rate in each of the years of the two or three previous generations of English people.

But from 1960 the rate of increase loses all comparison with the annual rates which had previously been the norm. In the following five years of exceptionally low unemployment, during what Bogdanor and Skidelsky called the age of affluence,[1] the rate rose to 2,600 per 100,000. The usual explanation was that people were less likely to behave themselves well when the money in their pockets removed the requirement that they must live their lives prudently. Low unemployment was particularly to blame for the rise in the crime rate. Why should a young man worry about his reputation, or even his criminal record, when he could walk with ease from one job to another? The only experience of the previous three generations was of the coincidence of high unemployment and insecure employment with what by the 1960s were recognized in retrospect as low and stable crime rates. When low unemployment and more secure employment coincided with sharply rising crime rates, the explanation that 'high unemployment causes crime', while at the time it had been a reasonable hypothesis of the cause of such crime as there was in the first half of the century, lost all its plausibility.

It was widely taken for granted that a delinquent from a home where there was no father (other than from the family of a dead man and his widow), in those days called without distinction a broken home, was automatically entitled to the court's sympathy. His was an obvious and proven delinquency-provoking background. Indeed, the home need only be 'broken' to the extent that a parent was not there when the child returned from school. The growth in juvenile crime, it was widely canvassed, was partly attributable to the deficiencies in supervision, and the lack of affection they felt their parents had for them, of 'latch-key children'.

By 1970 the rate of increase had brought the figure to 3,200 per 100,000. In 1980 the rate, 5,100 per 100,000, was ten times that which had been almost unchanged year by year from mid-Victorian times until just before the Second World War. Unemployment and Thatcherite greed were now the commonly attributed causes, together with (even though the material standard of living and housing standards were markedly higher than in the previous decades of low crime) poverty[2] and poor housing.[3]

The rate was 7,300 per 100,000 by 1985—over seven times the rate thirty years before. The rate in 1991, 10,000 per 100,000, was ten times what it had been in 1955, and the *rise* in the rate in the year 1990-91 was *twice* the *total* rate for the year 1955.

At the beginning of this century (1900-04) the total number of crimes recorded by the police in the whole of England and Wales ran at an annual average of just over 84,000. The rate was 258 per 100,000 population. At the beginning of the 1990s the number of crimes recorded by the police in a twelve-month period in one district of one city, the West End of Newcastle upon Tyne, was 13,500. The rate was one in three of the residents—33,000 per

100,000.[4] In the Sunderland of 1938 the bicycle, in number and as a working-class possession of value and means of transport, was roughly comparable to the motor car today. In the whole of that year, in the whole of the town, 50 were known by the police to have been stolen.[5] In the first six months of 1993 90 cars were stolen or broken into in Sunderland on a single car park of 197 spaces.[6]

If we take the figure for armed robbery, an offence the growth of which in the statistics could not be significantly accounted for by changes in reporting (more telephones, for example) and recording (changes in the law, changes in police procedures), we see that it was such a small problem that no figures were generally published until twenty years ago. In 1970 there were 480 armed robberies. By 1990 there were 3,900, and this rose in the following year to 5,300. This was an eleven-fold increase on 1970, and the increase in the single year was three times the total in 1970.[7] If we consider the total number, and not the rate of all cases of robbery, armed or not, the rise in England and Wales in the twelve months from 1990 to 1991 was two-and-a-half times all cases of robbery recorded in the entire period between the two world wars. These crimes were overwhelmingly the activity of young males. Any explanation of the rise in crime must therefore put at its centre that fact.

The other major change was in the activities of conceiving and rearing children. Thirty or forty years ago these were closely monitored by nearly every adult who came into contact with a mature couple. The intention was to ensure that, as far as possible, before a man had sexual intercourse with a woman, he should undertake far-reaching, long-lasting, and wide-ranging commitments to his possible child and the mother of his possible child. (It was not until the Lambeth Conference of 1930 that the bishops of the Church of England accepted that there could be 'a morally sound reason' for practising sexual intercourse *within marriage* when it could not lead to a child being conceived.) Binding obligations concerning procreation, child care, child rearing, and the type of care of adults for one another which could not be replaced from either professional or commercial sources, were required from the man within the social institution of the family. With increasing success and speed that control has been shaken off.

The man's duties towards his children and the mother of his children have been privatized—made into his own, from being a public affair—in three ways.

First, there has been an increase in the freedom for fathers (as there was for mothers) to leave their spouse, and for fathers to leave or lose their children. Legal changes—as always—were much less important than changes in public opinion. The law reached only a few crude externals of the immensely complicated, dense and fine-meshed web of British society's rules, expectations and practices touching on family conduct. These rules ranged from the ban on adultery to what was seemly language or scarcely perceptible gestures in a given situation. They were discussed and enforced, with variations, in Pall Mall clubs and pitmen's quoits games, in bourgeois suburb and corner shop. But changes in the law track and can stimulate (usually unpredicted and often undesired) changes in the complex and subtle (for all practical purposes, infinitely complex and subtle) social fabric of the time.

Up to the middle of the nineteenth century legal divorce was almost unknown in England. On any of several calculations the numbers were negligible. The Lord Chancellor's estimate in 1857 was that in the sixty years 1715 to 1775 there had been only sixty divorces. In the eighty-two years following, from 1775 to 1857, there had been two or three annually. Lawrence Stone found 17 divorces in the century 1650-1749. In the next half-century, to 1799, he estimated that there were a further 116. Bromley suggests there were about 200 divorces in the century 1757-1857. Joseph Jackson put the figure at 229.[8]

The divorce rate did not exceed 1,000 until 1914, and did not exceed 10,000 until 1942. In 1971, the first year of the operation of the Divorce Reform Act 1969, well over 100,000 new petitions were filed. Now there are well over 100,000 divorces a year where there are one or more children in the family.[9]

Socialization and social control, far more important than the law, were constantly losing their power to produce, and even the intention of producing, effective and successfully committed fathers. Women increasingly took the initiative in dismissing the fathers from their duties. They were judged so defective by their wives in one or more respects that the wives would rather have them fulfilling only those duties that could be discharged outside the matrimonial home, or no duties at all. By 1989 just under three-quarters of all new petitions were filed by the wife.[10]

Only 1 in 80 marriages celebrated in 1951 ended in divorce before the sixth anniversary. This was the case for one in nine of the couples married in 1981. For twenty years from 1961 the speed of this social change was 'truly dramatic', as the Family Policy Studies Centre put it.[11] In 1961 32,000 new petitions had been filed. In 1971 the figure had reached 111,000. In 1990 it was 192,000.[12] From being the country with one of the lowest rates of divorce in Europe among those with laws that permitted divorce, England became the country with the highest.[13]

Divorce rates only levelled out because a second and even more fundamental change took place. There was a marked growth in the number and proportion of couples who no longer regarded their private project of living together as requiring the formality even of the marriage that was nobody's business but their own. The man was less and less required by the woman, or anyone else in his social circles, to make a binding commitment to the possible mother of his children before he could have, without public censure and other penalties, regular sexual intercourse with her in a common household. This trend started with the cohabitation of couples who eventually married each other. In 1986-87 a sample of married women were asked whether they had cohabited with the man who was to become the husband of their first marriage. Of those married in 1966 only 2 per cent had thus cohabited before marriage. The proportion had tripled among the women marrying in 1971 to 7 per cent. It had nearly tripled again by 1976 to 19 per cent. By 1987 cohabitation before marriage had become almost the common as not cohabiting before marriage. For all marriages, not just first marriages, it had become commoner, and among married men much commoner (58 per cent).[14] Among a sample of nearly 11,500 people who were aged 33 on a certain day in 1991, 10 per cent were cohabiting at the time of the survey; about one third of those living with their first spouse had cohabited with the spouse before marriage; and 80 per cent had done so among those in their second or subsequent marriage.[15] By the 1990s 'partner' was the normal term by which the most staid organizations addressed even husbands and wives and 'current relationship' had become the euphemism for 'marital status' in social surveys.

The 1960s' hope, that 'trial marriages' would be the basis of greater stability when marriage was finally undertaken, has not been borne out by the facts. Marriages after cohabitation are more likely to end in divorce than marriages without prior cohabitation. Cohabitation is much more likely to end in lone parenthood than is marriage.[16] In recent years a new phenomenon has emerged; 'living together living apart'—i.e. sexual partners registering their own children together, but from separate addresses.[17]

The third change concerned something more than just two adults living together, namely, the domestic circumstances under which children would be born and brought up. It concerned especially the degree of certainty the child could enjoy that its father would be permanently committed to looking after it. During the first half of this century the percentage of births where the father had not committed himself by marriage remained at around 4 to 5 per cent, with the exception of the period around the time of both World Wars. During the Great War it peaked at 6 per cent. During World War II illegitimacy peaked at 9 per cent.[18] The ratio fell again after each period so that 'in the early 1950s the percentage of births outside marriage in the United Kingdom was still only slightly higher than it had been fifty years earlier'.[19]

In 1961 6 per cent of all births occurred without the man's having publicly committed himself to the child through marriage. In 1971 the figure was only sightly higher, 8 per cent. In 1981 it was still only 13 per cent. But in the 1980s children were born with ever-increasing frequency outside marriage, accounting by 1991 for over 30 per cent of all births, and among mothers born in the United Kingdom, for 32 per cent of all births.[20] Between 1986 and 1990 the number of never-married lone mothers almost doubled. Among all lone-parent families this was the group that was growing most rapidly, and in 1991 for the first time these unmarried father-absent situations formed a larger group than that of households headed by a divorced lone mother.[21] In 1961, where their mothers were under the age of 20, 53,000 babies had, and 13,000 had not, a publicly committed father. By 1989 the figures had almost exactly reversed, 13,000 with, and 48,000 without.

The number of births to teenagers rose rapidly to a peak in 1990. In 1991 83 per cent of all children born to teenagers were without a father committed to the child by marriage. If the recent study of pregnancy rates among females under the age of 20 admitted to NHS hospitals in the Tayside area for delivery or abortion between 1980 and 1990 gives an indication of the national situation, then fatherhood-free teenage siring is a feature of the lives of the women least able to cope with tasks of lone-parent child-rearing. The pregnancy rate was six times higher in the poorest areas of Tayside than in the most affluent areas. The pregnant teenagers from the least affluent areas were also less likely to have an abortion, and therefore more likely to have a sociologically fatherless baby.[22]

No man is a perfect father. Some men are the worst enemies of their wives and children. The separation of impregnation from pregnancy is a fact which allows the man to escape the consequences of procreation in a way and to a degree that is quite impossible for the woman. These things have always been true in all societies. What is new about ours is that the whole project of creating and maintaining the skills and motivations of fatherhood, and of imposing on men duties towards their own children that are as difficult as possible to escape, is being abandoned. What is more, for the first time in history on any large scale, the lead in requiring that the project be aborted has been taken by women.[23] Young men with a short-term view of life and hedonistic values have looked on with quiet delight, scarcely able to believe their luck. The adverse consequences of their sexual liberation do not fall, however, only on them.[24]

There is never any lack of reasons for our taking from others what law or custom says belongs to them, but which we know we are really entitled to. By our and we, I mean literally you and I. Nor is there ever any lack of reasons for venting our righteous anger in verbal and physical assaults on people who have unjustly given us less than our due in affection, income, honour, or career advancement; or on the premises of the firm for whom they work; or on the home and family of the rat who grassed on us; or randomly upon any property or persons in the society which has failed to give us our due. In that sense poor income, poor employment prospects, poor housing, or poor standing in one's workplace, at whatever standards that define what is 'poor', are the cause of crime, just as righteous territorial demands are the cause of aggressive wars and campaigns of ethnic cleansing.

The problem for people who want to live in peace and see their society increase in scale, efficiency and mutuality, constantly seeking the optimal adaptation of personal freedom to the common good, is how to handle these resentments in a constructive manner, whether as a family, a neighbourhood, a city, a nation or a whole world.

The consequences for children of dismantling sociological fatherhood have been documented by George Erdos and me in *Families Without Fatherhood*.[25] But there are consequences that are even more profound and which reach far beyond the child in the family without fatherhood. Only some boys and girls today are children from father-absent families. But all boys and young men without exception—whether they are one month old or ten years old or twenty-five years old—face their future with progressively reducing social pressure or social training to become responsible and competent husbands and fathers. By training I do not mean the blunt instrument of formal lessons.[26] Fatherhood is learned like a language. It is assimilated like one's native tongue or not at all. It is transmitted through the countless messages of reinforcement and restriction that come every day, from the moment of birth, through parents, other kinsfolk, neighbours, and passing strangers. These messages embody, like one's native tongue, the common sense of generations, derived from the experience of ordinary people as well as the contributions of geniuses, of what has proved benign and practicable in everyday life.

That is not a doctrine of 'a Golden Age'. It is the doctrine of problems presented and perennially re-presented by human nature. It is the doctrine that maintaining an equitable pattern of rights and duties is infinitely more difficult than devising one. It is the doctrine that sometimes these stubborn problems have been partly solved. In societies fortunate in their intellectuals, such solutions that have proven humane and decent in practice have been retained. In dealing specifically with the man's conduct in sexual relations and child rearing, it is the doctrine of holding on to any hard-won progress. This has occurred if and when our parents and grandparents, and their parents and grandparents, have been lucky enough to inherit a language of fatherhood capable of being improved upon, and when they have been wise and competent enough to improve it.

The real doctrine of the 'mythical Golden Age' is that of the Golden Age of present practices and values, which dismisses as worthless, where they were not malignant, the values and practices of their own fathers, grandfathers and great-grandfathers; or when that is put to them directly, other people's fathers, grandfathers and great-grandfathers.

If we are looking for something that has profoundly changed for young males in the twenty or thirty years during which many of them have gone on the rampage, it is not increasing poverty. We have become richer. It is not a deteriorating housing stock. Housing has been progressively improved. It is not high unemployment. The trend of the crime rate has been upward through periods of low unemployment. It is in the social definition of what it is to be a mature man, and social definition is partly the work of a society's intellectuals. Their work is always slow in helping to create a culture, but can be swift in dismantling it. Under modern conditions of mass communication and entertainment the undermining of other people's hard-won culture by pressure-group propaganda is their facile and enduring achievement; they can easily destroy what it passes their wit to rebuild.

2

The Individualizing and Rationalizing Intelligentsia

As C. Wright Mills insisted, in modern complex societies we all live to a greater or lesser extent in second-hand worlds; and these worlds are to a greater or lesser extent constructed for us by those who seek and are given access to the channels through which powerful impulses of persuasion can flow. The quality of our lives is determined by meanings we have received from others, and 'no man stands alone directly confronting a world of solid fact'. To be a sociologist, he said, was to accept that as a datum.[1] The intellectual, living or dead, is the effective definer of the facts (what are to be regarded as the facts) of past, present and future situations. The intellectual is the effective definer, also, of the appropriate response, i.e. the moral response, to the facts so defined.

Some sociologists, therefore, have seen it as being one of their most important tasks to explore the world-view of intellectuals who are involved in these activities of description and judgement. The very limited and modest aim of these sociologists, and if you like their trawl in very shallow waters, is to explain only in the sense of describing the intentions of the actor, and the actor's personal view of the facts and ethics of his present situation. It is 'explanation', that is, limited to understanding or interpretation. The theory that conduct depends on the one hand upon the actors' subjective perception of the facts about their objective situation, and on the other upon their beliefs about how they should react to what they believe their situation to be (i.e. their values), is linked in its modern sociological forms with the name of the German sociologist Max Weber. To avoid disputes about what the words interpretation and understanding are to mean in these contexts the key word for both them is often left in the German: *das Verstehen*; *verstehende* sociology. 'We can accomplish something that is never attainable in the natural sciences, namely the subjective understanding of the action of the component individuals.'[2]

The sociology of understanding is based upon the assumption that human beings are fundamentally different from any other object of investigation in this respect (at any rate in degree if not as compared with some higher, non-human, animals in kind): they have a highly developed capacity to imagine quite complicated future states of affairs. What is possible in the future, being necessarily unknowable, frees the human being to an unusual extent from the facts of the case. But what is also peculiar and crucial is the capacity and indeed strong propensity of human beings to base their conduct upon these imagined future states of affairs.

To a lesser but still very considerable extent a peculiarity of human beings is their ability to base their conduct upon possibly quite fanciful perceptions of what the facts of the present situation are, from which they must start on their project of realizing their intentions. Closely related to that, human beings possess a peculiar capacity to communicate possibly fanciful accounts both of what the future can hold, and of what is true in the present. They can do this innocently and authentically, in which case (if they are wrong) they are acting under an illusion (at the extreme they are mentally ill). Or they can do it inauthentically, in which case we say they are lying.

Interpretative sociology believes in the superiority of statements based upon methods ('scientific' methods) designed to minimize as far as possible the human tendency to believe whatever suits one at the time. That is what Weber meant, and that is the only thing that he meant, when he said that this type of sociology is value-free.

It applies scientific methods only to descriptions of the various empirically-existing constellations of beliefs about the facts, and the various empirically-existing moral judgements upon those conjectured facts. These descriptions are not in themselves assessments by the sociologist on the accuracy of the facts or judgements on the validity of the morals of the world-view studied. The task of the interpretative sociologist is limited to the understanding, in the Weberian sense of the term, of the particular world-view or world-views under investigation, on the merits of which she or he remains, as sociologist, neutral. 'Whirl is King, having driven out

Zeus.' A reasonable contribution of sociology—of Weberian sociology—was to make some sense of the components of that whirl.

Weber insisted, further, that it was not for sociologists to abuse their position in the lecture hall and impose their own view of the facts and least of all their own values or lack of them on their students. That, he said, was an 'outrage'. For the words of the sociologist as academic are then 'not plough-shares to loosen the soil of contemplative thought; they are swords against their enemies'.

But most of all he insisted that outside the lecture hall, on a level playing-field of debate, the sociologist as citizen is not prohibited from saying what she or he thinks of the version of the facts or epistemological relativity presented by others, and the system of morality or moral nihilism implied in their statements and silences. Quite the contrary: 'to come out clearly and take a stand is one's damned duty'.[3]

What has been the social role generally of the intellectual in the urban-industrial world?

In the eighteenth century the new social-affairs intellectuals played the role recommended by Edward Said in the first of the BBC Reith Lectures 1993: that of the disrupter of the current consensus. The ideas of the eighteenth-century dissenters from the monarchical and clerical consensus, the ideas of the Enlightenment, became the intellectual consensus of the West in the nineteenth century.

Social-affairs intellectuals in the nineteenth century shared the very widespread belief in the inevitability of improvement in human conduct and social cooperation. What had happened to the most favoured sections of the populations of Western Europe and the United States, technologically and socially, would eventually happen all over the world.

Reformist social-affairs intellectuals foresaw the continuous and peaceful but nevertheless rapid spread of these advantages.[4] Progressive revolutionary doctrines foresaw an imminent transformation of the advanced industrial nations with all their existing riches unequally distributed, into societies of generalized plenty. In these revolutionary doctrines (the most important of which proved, of course, to be Marxism) the administration of things would abruptly replace the government of men. Freed from the necessity to work as employees by modern technology and by the just distribution of its products, people would engage in useful or aesthetic activities for the joy which creative activity gives the human being as such, and especially for the joy of creative activity for the benefit of others. The rough climb which had constituted the pre-history of humankind would be completed on the high plateau of a changeless, everlastingly peaceable, egalitarian and altruistic utopia.[5]

Until the 'revolt against reason' at the end of the nineteenth and beginning of the twentieth centuries—let me mention Nietzsche and Sorel[6]—the major postulate in all of these progressive reformist and revolutionary doctrines was that more and more people would base their conduct on rationally- and logically-based perceptions of, and moral judgements upon, their physical and social world and their own position within it. Progress, on this view, both depended upon and would foster scientific modes of thought. In sociology the synonym 'positivistic' was often substituted for 'scientific'.[7] The definition of the factual and moral situation would incrementally come to correspond to 'real' reality, by giving cognizance only to those facts and theories which for the time being had withstood the most rigorous exposure to empirical investigation, and responses to 'real' reality would be increasingly just and benign.

Superstition, the medieval fantasies of received religion, and the reactionary dreams of restoring the sanctified social order of feudalism were as far from the mainstream of thought as was the extreme libertarianism of Max Stirner's *The Ego and Its Own*.[8] It was the age of reason.[9]

The social basis of Western societies was visibly and incontrovertibly being transformed from community to association; from the solidarity that stems from similarity to solidarity that stems from the division of differential labour; from cooperation between people defined by their unchangeable statuses, to cooperation between people joined and separated as parties to mutually convenient contracts.

As the twentieth century progressed it became obvious that modern social conditions were not forcing rational and logical

13

perceptions upon the intelligentsia. On the contrary, the freedom from famine, plague, and rapine afforded for considerable periods in the most favoured of the industrialized and urbanized countries increasingly disclosed itself as a breeding-ground for not only the most diverse perceptions of reality and conceptions of what constitutes good and evil conduct, but for philosophies which denied that there were better or worse versions of the truth, and better or worse modes of social conduct. With plentiful supplies of food, clothing, shelter, health care and so forth, the illusion could begin to flourish that this was a permanent and guaranteed condition.

For discrete individuals (and *a fortiori* for comfortably-off intellectuals), as distinct from all individuals in the long term, the painful consequences of failing to test assumptions and predictions against actual occurrences—the failure to exercise adequately the great human capacity of common sense which, as Arendt said, is nothing but our mental organ for perceiving, understanding, and dealing with reality and factuality[10]—were now greatly mitigated. Notions about the faults of such societies were free to proliferate in ignorance of, or even with scorn for rational and logical modes of investigation and argument. We are reminded once again of Proudhon's passing remark on 'the fecundity of the unexpected', which far exceeds not only the statesman's prudence, but also the predictive powers of social science.

Surprisingly (surprisingly if nineteenth century assumptions had any substance) within their cocoon of riches social-affairs intellectuals did not move uniformly towards greater rationality. The results of human action, as distinct from the end-products of fabrication, had patently escaped the nineteenth century's bold efforts at reliable prediction.

Weberian sociology itself developed out of the recognition of the new conditions under which the intellectual was now defining the factual and moral situation. As I have observed above, it itself adhered firmly to the nineteenth-century faith in the superiority of scientific, positivistic, procedures as a way of bringing perceptions into line with hard reality. But it took for granted neither continuous progress nor, specifically, the growing dominance of rational investigation and logical argument generally.

Cutting across this classification of the intelligentsia transmitting the heritage of the Enlightenment as against the emerging pessimistic and non- or anti-scientific intelligentsia, was the classification that depended on an intellectual's theory of social causation.

One tradition stems from Marxism, and gives primacy, where it does not give an exclusive place, to material influences on human conduct. 'In the social production of their lives', as Marx wrote in a familiar and emphatic passage, 'men enter into relations that are indispensable and independent of their will', and these indispensable relations, outside any individual's sphere of choice, are created by the necessities of utilizing to the full the existing means of the production of material necessities. People's perception of what is factually true and their judgement of what is morally appropriate do not determine their response to their material conditions. Their material conditions determine both the how they will perceive their world and what their morality will be. 'It is not the consciousness of men that determines their being, but, on the contrary, their social being that determines their consciousness.'[11]

Of course this doctrine has been interpreted in many ways in different societies and at different times. The materialist doctrine has slowly soaked through and dried out of many progressive layers. After 134 years it has, for example, at last reached some of the most conservative layers of all, and appears, at the moment of its general expiry, in the Church of England in its most debased form, in the proposition that crime is caused by poverty, bad housing and unemployment.[12]

Applied to family life, a modern version of the Marxist argument is that while families 'mutate symbiotically' with economic demands and prospects, economic demands and prospects are dominant as explanatory factors in change. Thus, the early industrial economy 'needed' child labour and mobile, expendable young males. Therefore big, flexible households resulted. The maturing industrial economy 'required' a steadier, well-drilled proletariat. Therefore women and children were ushered out of the labour force, and husbands '"employed" wives at the kitchen sink'. Contemporary capitalism creates jobs for women 'because they are cheaper and more tractable'. Therefore the fatherless family becomes the norm, in which it is quite unrealistic to expect young mothers to shoulder the burden of husbands as well as the burden of their infants. The shift from the disorderly working-class family of 1800 to the sober, respectable working-class 'unit' [sic] of 1950 was 'essentially' a response to economic change, not itself a significant moral originator of economic success or failure, as is the shift to the household of the father-absent child. There will continue to be 'families' though under forms we cannot yet foresee; and these forms will be shaped by the economy.[13]

The theory of materialistic causality is not linked particularly closely with the nineteenth-century tradition of inevitable progress. Many of the comprehensive theories of progress were predicated upon the evolution of Spirit (Hegel),[14] the Mind (Comte)[15] or Morals (Hobhouse).[16]

But the second theory of causality in social life as morality is closely linked with the Weberian tradition of interpretative sociology. Weber himself did not claim to know whether 'ultimately', 'in the long run', and so forth, material forces dominated the development of human character and the patterns of social cooperation and conflict. All he proposed was that it could be decisively shown that, for at least periods long enough to be of very high relevance to actual, living human beings (for a generation or more) different sets of people confronted with the same material conditions reacted to them in distinctly different ways. Their different reactions depended upon their conception of the desirable future (their intentions) and upon their factual and moral perceptions of their present situation.

From about 1900 to about 1965 conventional sociology as it developed in the United States, France and Germany, and as it developed more weakly in this country (in the later years of the period, as an outpost of American sociology), was centred on this notion of the importance of a person's and of course collectivity's definition of the situation, factual and moral, as the key to social explanation. If people define situations as real, they are real in their consequences.[17]

The emphasis laid by the French sociologist Durkheim, as well as the German sociologist Weber, on the importance of the *moral assessment* of what people *believed the facts of the case to be* greatly impressed Talcott Parsons,[18] the man who was to become the principal architect of American sociology before it was superseded with remarkable rapidity in the late 1960s by various forms of Marxist sociology. Durkheim's first statement in the Preface to the first edition of *The Division of Labour in Society* is that the book is above all an attempt to treat the facts of the moral life by the method of the positive sciences.[19]

As is the case with all sociologists, Durkheim's interest was not so much—or in his case at all—in the individualized ethic of the single individual, but in the ensemble of beliefs and sentiments shared by a set of people. That a set of people do hold the same set of values is the thing, and the only thing, that makes them a social group. A group cannot exist on the basis of individual interests alone, least of all individual material interests, and material interests cannot on their own operate as an effective driving force of successful social cooperation.

From the very beginning of the documentation of his thought in the last decade of the nineteenth century, Durkheim was deeply concerned with the role of moral values and, specifically, shared moral values, in determining individual and group action. The line which Durkheim took in *The Division of Labour* was that individualistic doctrines such as *laissez faire*, and materialistic doctrines such as Marxism, failed to take account of the elements which actually are to be found in the existing system of transactions.

This was true even in the strongest individualist case, the supposedly purely self-interested transactions of the market place. For Durkheim the utilitarian contract was the prototype of the individualist and materialist relationship: in utilitarian theory's crudest form, the mutual advantage derived by the parties from the various exchanges was considered to be the principal cohesive force of the system.

What was omitted, said Durkheim, was the fact that these transactions are actually entered into in accordance with a body of binding rules which existed prior to the ad hoc agreement of the parties. Without a complex of beliefs and sentiments which formed the social institution of contract, the system of free exchange between individuals or groups simply could not exist.

Legal rules were necessary to regulate what contracts were and what were not valid. Legal rules regulated the means by which the

parties' assent to the contract could be obtained: an agreement secured by fraud or under duress was void. They regulated various consequences of a contract once made, both to the parties them- selves and to third persons. Legal rules regulated, finally, the procedure by which contracts could be enforced.

But the agreed definition of the situation, constituted by a set of people in the laws to which they give their assent, by no means stood alone. If the laws underpinning the system of individualized exchange were to be effective, they themselves had to be supple- mented by a vast body of customary rules which were obligatory equally with the laws, even though they were not enforceable in the courts.

All this applied par excellence to the family, but was hardly discussed in relation to it, because the family's safety and perma- nence as an institution were taken so much for granted by the sociologists of the time, both in Europe and the United States. The possibility of the privatization of the family was hardly ever considered.[20]

In the middle of the nineteenth century no one expressed more clearly or pungently than Marx did the idea that modern society destroys these agreed definitions of the factual and moral situation.

> Uninterrupted disturbance of all social conditions, everlasting uncer- tainty and agitation distinguish the bourgeois epoch from all others. All fixed, fast frozen relations with their train of ancient and venerable prejudices and opinions are swept away, all new-formed ones become antiquated before they can ossify. All that is solid melts in the air, all that is holy is profaned ...

Modern urban-industrial society had changed personal worth into exchange value. It had stripped the halo from every activity hitherto honoured and looked up to with reverent awe, and drowned the most heavenly ecstasies of religious fervour and chivalrous enthusiasm 'in the icy waters of egoistical calculation'.[21] For the Marx of *The Communist Manifesto* the result would be the creation of a community of rational beings by the victorious proletariat in a communist society.

A century later Schumpeter made Marx's negative point again, but omitted altogether Marx's buoyant view of the sequel. Unlike any other type of society, Schumpeter wrote, ours 'inevitably and by the very logic of its civilization' creates, educates and subsidizes a class of specialists in social unrest. In Schumpeter's view, this key position was occupied by the intelligentsia, the people who wielded the power of the spoken and the written word in the absence of any direct responsibility for practical affairs. Urban-industrial societies did indeed produce their own grave-diggers, but these were its intellectuals, not its workers, and there was no resurrection for the corpse.

Ordinary people going about their ordinary business did not change a society's ways of perceiving and evaluating reality. Pre-eminently this was not true of any 'underclass'. Neither the opportunity to attack institutions such as the family, nor real or fancied grievances against such institutions, were themselves sufficient to produce, however strongly they might favour, the emergence of widespread and active hostility against them. For such an atmosphere to develop it is necessary that there be specialized intellectuals whose interest it is to work up and organize resentment, to nurse it, to voice it and to lead it. In modern societies, conditions favourable to general hostility to a social system, or attacks upon specific institutional areas like kinship, would call forth an intelligentsia that would exploit them.[22]

Schumpeter was particularly pessimistic about the power of scientifically-based information and common-sense appeals to everyday experience as a corrective to the destructive work of the intellectual. It was true, he said, that the fashion-following intellectuals' criticism of a particular social institution, and of social order as an ideal, proceeded from a desacralizing attitude of mind. That is, it was an attitude that spurned allegiance to any notion of the sacred, any notion of the role of extra-rational values, of unquestioned other-regardingness, in ensuring social cohesion. But it did not follow that rational refutation would be accepted by these social critics. Rational refutation could tear away the rational garb of the conforming intellectuals' attack, but it could never reach the extra-rational driving power always lurking behind these attacks: their personal interests in untrammelled self-expression, fame and money. Their rationality does not do away with their sub- or super-rational impulses:

It merely makes them get out of hand by removing the restraint of sacred or semi-sacred tradition. In a civilization that lacks the means or even the will to control these impulses they will revolt. And once they revolt it matters little that, in a rationalist culture, their manifestations will in general be somehow 'rationalized'.[23]

The institution under scrutiny, be it church, royalty, business firm, parliament, police or family, stood its trial before judges who had the sentence of death already in their pockets.

3

The English Intelligentsia and the Civility of Everyday Life Until the Nineteen-Sixties

What has been the view of, specifically, the English social-affairs intellectual to, specifically, the civility of everyday life in England?

The civilities of everyday life had for long remained relatively immune from the debunking of the fashion-following intellectual elite. Until the early 1960s the view was consensual among intellectuals and non-intellectuals that everyday social disorder was bad, and that England in particular had been blessed for many years with an unusually law-abiding population.

For example, in 1944 George Orwell wrote approvingly of the 'gentle-mannered, undemonstrative, law-abiding English':

> An imaginary foreign observer would certainly be struck by our gentleness; by the orderly behaviour of English crowds, the lack of pushing and quarrelling ...And except for certain well-defined areas in half-a-dozen big towns, there is very little crime or violence.[1]

A few years later a noted anthropologist, Geoffrey Gorer, set out the problem he had to solve if he were to give an adequate account of the English national character. 'In public life today', he wrote,

> the English are certainly among the most peaceful, gentle, courteous and orderly populations that the civilized world has ever seen ... the control of aggression has gone to such remarkable lengths that you hardly ever see a fight in a bar (a not uncommon spectacle in most of the rest of Europe or the USA), [and] football crowds are as orderly as church meetings.

Still in 1955 it was this, to use Gorer's words, 'orderliness, gentleness, and absence of overt aggression' that puzzled the anthropologist and called for an explanation.[2]

K.B. Smellie, a professor at the London School of Economics respected by and popular with the students of the late 1940s and early 1950s—his version of the Englishman of the time was not the subject of indignant disbelief—wrote of him [and her] that:

> The life of the town has given him a discipline which is unsurpassed because for the most part self-imposed and which has made him amenable and loyal to sensible leadership in new conditions or in any emergency. The pattern of life in a wartime air raid shelter was as orderly as that of the group of pilgrims in Chaucer's *Canterbury Tales*.

(If in the 1940s or 1950s there had been a breakdown of social order, and a steep rise in the crime and violence among and from young men, there would have been no difficulty in accepting without question that, more than adequately, social theory identified the inevitable and irresistible causes of burgeoning crime and violence as the war and its aftermath—and the second war and the second aftermath within the space of thirty years at that. *That* would have been a reasonable basis for a consensus among social-affairs intellectuals. But there was no breakdown in social order, and no crime wave.)

Smellie continues:

> There can be little doubt that the life of towns has steadily improved. ... Drunkenness has fallen steadily. So too has public violence. ... From the Yahoo habits of eighteenth-century London we have passed into an almost Houyhnhnm rationality of orderly processions and patient queues. And, almost certainly with the passing of violence, drunkenness and squalor, has gone much cruelty as well. Personal relations are more gentle and, as one observer has said 'the contemporary English would appear to have as unaggressive a public life as any recorded people'.[3]

Richard Hoggart, in contemplating in 1957 the future of the English working class under the impact of the new conditions for the creation of public opinion, has no presentiment at all that crime rates would dramatically increase within the next few years, or that the family as he knew it would be transformed. Rather (he quoted Tocqueville) there was the danger of deterioration into 'a kind of virtuous materialism', which would 'not corrupt, but enervate the soul, and noiselessly unbend the springs of action'.[4]

It is equally striking that as late as 1962 Carstairs' BBC Reith Lectures, *This Island Now*, another summary of the state of the nation, shows no awareness that crime was a problem in England. He takes for granted throughout, and explicitly states, that England's high degree of civility was a rare achievement for the rest of the world to emulate. As far as the family is concerned, he does have some things to say which show that he held the view that was about to become consensual among the progressive intelligentsia for a short while, that the family of the publicly-committed father and mother would be *stronger* if the trends to free it from the constraints of law and custom were intensified and accelerated.[5]

1962 was the year that R.H. Tawney died. In our *English Ethical Socialism* Professor Halsey and I make much of that date and that event, for Tawney, too, died secure in the belief that the British welfare state for which he had worked for a lifetime would be the buttress of the best features of the Britain, especially the England of which he was so proud, including its internal civil peace and the strength of its family life.[6]

The physical scene helped reinforce this consensus (right or wrong) of fact and value. As Richard Clutterbuck reminds us, the first time that an English policeman was equipped with as much as a perspex riot shield was in the confrontation between the Socialist Workers' Party and the National Front at Lewisham, south London, in August 1977.[7]

A certain German politician was recently reported as supporting '"Law and Order" ... Dies heiße Gesetz und Recht ... '[8] The concept of an orderly society of law and justice, lightly controlled because willingly accepted, remains in English, as having no equivalent in German, just as in German 'der Sport' and 'das Fair play', 'gentle-manlike' and 'das Gentlemen's Agreement' remain in English. I was once on a walking tour in the Eifel district, and met a German on the outskirts of a village near Aachen. He said he had been a prisoner of war in 'Luton Town'. I said that I hoped he had been well treated. He replied, in German, 'Ein Engländer ist fair'.

In the last twenty years the untranslatable words that have entered the German language in English are 'der Rowdy', 'der Skinhead' and, to be seen scribbled by Germans on the walls of Cologne Cathedral, those of obscene, aggressive and deliberately anti-social discourse. In Westphalia I walked into the neat little town of Werl, thinking perhaps that its streets had rarely been trodden by foreign foot. A notice on the window of the first public house I came to said, 'English people not served'.

People who had not benefited from giving or attending courses in post-1970 sociology, depended upon what they read straight-forwardly reported in the local newspaper.[9] They depended upon their crude general impression from everyday life. They experienced, for example, criminal events themselves that they thought were not experienced to the same degree by previous generations in this century; they witnessed metal shutters gradually being installed in all shopping centres; they saw high fences being erected for the first time around vandalized and defaced churches, and so forth. Among them there remained a wide consensus that civility in England and Wales had significantly declined in the previous thirty years. Their own experience, that is, corresponded with the statistical records.

But under the persistent contrary message of the serious media based on the world-view of the metropolitan intelligentsia (a message that constituted a sustained assault on common sense) the consensus was at its most insecure and weakest among the best informed sections of the community, and especially among those well informed sections who were geographically at farthest remove from the areas where the impact of crime and vandalism most heavily fell.

4

The English Intelligentsia and the Civility of Everyday Life Since the Nineteen-Sixties

Since the 1960s the social-affairs intelligentsia has not shared the consensus of the ill-informed, at least until very recently—literally until a few months or even weeks ago.

What Patricia Morgan called 'the enlightened response' to crime statistics was to dismiss them with scorn. The increase in crime was a statistical mirage (did anyone ever say, a *fata morgana*?) that misled only simpletons. The enlightened response to the popular consensus was to mock it as 'moral panic'; the public was not responding rationally to a growth in criminal conduct, it was reacting to 'images of deviance'.[1] All that could be derived from the statistics was that they had risen; crime and other forms of social disorder had not.

One of the contradictions of this point view was that, if the statistics were useless, and there was therefore only personal experience to go by, from what factual sources did the members of the orthodox intelligentsia derive their confidence that it was others who were panicking, and not they who were being complacent?

The interesting question for the enlightened intelligentsia, then, was to reveal the dark motives, as again Patricia Morgan remarked, of those who manufacture these statistics, which show a rise in crime when there has been no real rise. A common answer until recently was that they reflected only rising official attempts to expand the personnel engaged in state repression.

Other sections of the conforming social-affairs intelligentsia shared the viewpoint given by common sense and the statistical record as to the facts of the loss of English civility, but differed from ordinary people in the moral interpretation of that loss. I have dealt with this point at length elsewhere.[2] But a fairly recent issue of the *Architects' Journal* expresses this view so well I shall quote it here.

25

Much more important than the fact that someone had written these passages—as with other similar examples in this essay—is the fact that the article was published by an organ of opinion controlled by and appealing to the society's elite. There is no question of everything that everyone says or writes being publicized. The quality of the intellectual life of a society can be assessed from the quality and content of the materials that are granted an audience and accorded prestige and credence by what the great William Cobbett called 'our best public instructors'.

The author is castigating what he calls the 'New Victorians' for wishing to control crime and social disorder, and who define 'crime' vaguely 'as a code word for anyone who threatens the "stable society" or who offends against "civilized standards"' —concepts the author places in quotation marks.

> The petrol bomber, the graffiti artist and the 'vandal' are lumped together with the mugger, the rapist and child molester, perhaps because it would play havoc with the statistics to redefine some of these criminals as rebels, or even free spirits.

No doubt the New Victorians, the author continues, will 'scientifically' prove that it is the frustrated poor, the frustrated ethnic groups and the frustrated blacks, who seem most prone to crime and riot in England. 'So great efforts are made to ... return us all to some mythical social stability.'

Having in one breath dismissed social stability as a myth, because he feels such abhorrence for it he immediately reinstates it as a fact in order to ridicule it.

> Like all good Victorians, they choose to believe that if the masses would only wash and go to Sunday School they would be happier. ...Well, it worked in the past and it may work again, particularly if the real goal is, as I suspect, to recreate the 'virtuous poor'—another classic Victorian concept—the virtuous poor who inhabited the cosy (though decrepit) streets of pre-war Britain .. They look fondly upon the old communities where 'children were taught to respect private property' and where society was 'stable'. ... But we were virtuous because, in the eyes of our social rulers we behaved ourselves; we did not spread graffiti everywhere, nor vandalize our neighbour's 'castle' and we most certainly had a healthy respect (even adulation) for authority of any kind ... We almost took pride in ... the fact that 'you could eat your dinner off the

floor of the outside lavatory' ... We were like that because we were ignorant—centuries of the British method of social control ensured that.

Crime and disorder, on this world-view, have risen—but that is a good, not a bad thing. For now, he continues, 'the child (the new, informed generation) perhaps turns the despair into anger and ends up throwing a petrol bomb, being then branded a "criminal"'.

It is thus clear and admirable that new generations have emerged who have realized that the old ways were 'a confidence trick played on the poor and disadvantaged'. To these newer generations litter dropping is, commendably, not a 'lapse in social behaviour' to be 'corrected' but (presumably) an heroic act of defiance. The author expresses his agreement with Oscar Wilde, that the virtues of the poor were much to be regretted. The 'most far-sighted among the communities of our dreadful estates are probably the ungrateful, the disobedient, and rebellious'.[3]

Clearly, something very profound and new had happened when the social-affairs intelligentsia turned its desacralizing and individualizing criticism on the family and crime. For it was no longer a critique based on individualism as such. It was now a critique based upon a highly self-centred and hedonistic individualism; and upon an individualism not of the person's reason, but of his emotions and will.

The disruption of the consensus on crime that the intelligentsia had shared with the common people was already evident in France and the United States in the late 1950s, as various writers began their flirtation with drugs and sexual liberation. In France this occurred as a reaction to the Second World War and its aftermath of Cold War and colonial defeats, and under the banner of an elitist existentialism. In America it occurred as a reaction against McCarthyism and the ever-present threat of nuclear war, with the highly male-chauvinistic Beats and hipsters playing what seemed at the time the unlikely role of exemplars for their generation.[4]

But the main disruption came ten years later, at the time of the students' international rebellion against 'mass society'. This had been triggered by the enormous growth of student campuses at the time of major historical events, such as America's involvement in the Vietnam War; the emergence of new leaders and new techniques in the American civil-rights movement; and movements for

27

freedom from Western colonialism elsewhere in the world, which by the 1960s came to be heavily influenced by the notion propagated by, for example, Frantz Fanon, that in freeing himself from oppression, personally murdering the oppressor (the ultimate expression of emotion and will) was for the individual 'a cleansing force'.[5]

The tendency to make law-breaker and hero all but interchangeable terms in popular language has been a common feature of societies clearly split into oppressors and oppressed, whether between Norman and Anglo-Saxon in England in the thirteenth, or Serb and Ottoman Turk in the Balkans in the nineteenth,[6] or peasant and French settler in Algeria in the twentieth century. Only under modern conditions, however, does the temper of the times encourage a rich and parliamentary society's intellectuals to identify themselves on a large scale with the law-breaking of their own oppressed, and not only to champion lawlessness against tyrannous regimes abroad—a common national response in all societies—but also to advocate that it should be at least exonerated when used by or on behalf of the 'relatively deprived' at home.

The mature intellectual or the student in rich and stable countries like Britain and the United States could afford to apply these Stirnerian and Dostoyevskian interpretations of reality to her or his own condition, because they were without significant adverse consequences for her or him.[7] People for whom there were significant consequences from increasing crime and other expressions of incivility, in the form of the steep deterioration in the quality of their neighbourhood life, remained much more firmly anchored in their own first-hand experiences. The figures quoted in Chapter 1 for Newcastle's West End refer to crimes committed within this once working-class, now 'deprived' area. The crimes are not righteous rampages against the rich, or burglaries from the dwellings of those who have ground the faces of the poor. They are an aspect of the much wider breakdown of civility among young males which had made everyday life very unpleasant for residents in the area, and those who have not already been made victims feel that they are just 'waiting their turn'.[8]

As Said remarked in the BBC Reith Lecture referred to above, the intellectual's obligation is to be the spokesman for the poor—the intellectual as Robin Hood, as he put it (thus revealing his own conformity with, not dissent from, the consensus of the social-affairs intelligentsia, not least importantly with that part of it employed in the post-Reithian BBC). This had been the dominant philosophy of the leaders of the movements of student unrest of the late 1960s and early 1970s. No-one but the permanent critic of society can be a genuine social-affairs intellectual. Whenever they are willing to emerge from their natural element, which is unremitting criticism, intellectuals become 'mere means at the disposal of the existing order'. When a social statement takes the form of affirmation, its truth evaporates.[9]

Even more far-reaching in its significance, important sections of the desacralizing and individualizing intelligentsia now based its critique upon the rejection of scientific modes of thought. The rebellious student leaders were very much influenced by the anti-positivism of such writers as Marcuse, Horkheimer and Adorno. The application of scientific method to the study of human affairs was not the route to the solution of social problems; on the contrary, the problems of society were due to 'the present triumph of the factual mentality'.[10] The immediate and obvious illustration of this was the apparently disastrous results of applying the 'rational' principles of the RAND corporation to the conduct of the war in Vietnam.[11] Positivism, since the time of Comte sociology's proudest motto, became under the influence of the so-called Critical Sociologists a wide-ranging, severe, and all-purpose term of disapprobation. 'Facticity' was one of the 'tyrannies' that had to be broken.

Only the intellectual who sides with the deprived (the word itself begs the fundamental question), on their terms (judgementalism is banned), can be correct on the facts and sound in his morality; therefore adherence to the cause of the politically-correct advocacy group is crucial, not loyalty to scientific procedures. No superficially plausible facts that undermines the case of the deprived, as they define their own case, can be ultimately true. In its most unintelligent form, it appears as a vague notion that good intentions are more important than sound scholarship—a kind of pallid left-wing version of red-necked know-nothingism.

The intellectual justification for this mind-set (and even the terms themselves, positivism and anti-positivism), have faded from discussion since their militant hey-day in the early 1970s. Hostility to awkward facts is no longer underpinned by a grandiose if implausible metaphysics nor enunciated in a high flown if opaque literary style. It merely lingers as a naive prejudice. By the 1980s anti-positivism was a residue rather than a deliberately-chosen and defended position. It was no longer studied as a philosophy, but unreflectively imbibed as the prevailing fashion.

So long as the anti-positivistic consensus in social affairs remained more or less unbroken these lapses of memory presented few problems either to academic intellectuals, or to the intellectuals in charitable foundations and government bureaucracies who supported their work, or to the intellectuals in the media who disseminated their views.

But this history explains why, when they are now challenged to address positivistic data on their merits, and are asked to reconcile their convictions with the brute facts of the case, and not just the tame facts collected in abundance, their intellectual performance is so feeble. They know neither how to justify their anti-positivistic stance, nor how to handle inconvenient research findings. They flounder around with figures they despise, and which they have therefore never taken the trouble to master. This is what has in recent years turned the political left into what it long accused the political right of being: the Stupid Party.

The individualizing and rationalizing social-affairs intelligentsia had been notably harsh on the proletarian and lumpen-proletarian criminal—as harsh as was Marx himself.[12] The individualizing and anti-positivistic social-affairs intelligentsia of the 1970s and 1980s, who perceived and evaluated him either as victim of oppression or rebellious hero, was notably well-disposed towards him. Simple analogies were drawn between colonialism and 'internal colonialism'. What was to be condemned in the ordinary crimes and rampages of the oppressed and deprived in England, when the 'cleansing violence' of anti-colonialism was more or less standard doctrine?

Marcuse laid his hopes for a better society with the 'substratum of the outcasts and outsiders' which 'violates the rules of the game and, in doing so, reveals that it is a rigged game'. This substratum will act as the liberator of the 'conservative popular base', by revealing to it its 'false consciousness'—the terrible error made by ordinary people that modern welfare-state democracies are benign. The problem was not to tame the barbarians within them, for the true barbarism was 'the continued empire of civilization itself'.[13] The deviant is no longer the proper object of society's control. She or he is society's saviour. In the 1970s and into the 1980s, the superiority of the world-view of the criminal over that of the law-abiding citizen became the stock-in-trade of the dominant New Criminology[14] and Critical Sociology.[15]

The fate of two-year-old James Bulger, abducted by two ten-year-old boys from the New Strand shopping centre at Bootle on 12 February 1993 and allegedly murdered, caused a world-wide sensation[16] and probably dealt the death blow to the 'moral panic' school. Again, a pernicious theory and a cant phrase were given what was perhaps their last airing by conservative elements such as clergymen interesting enough to be interviewed on the radio, to whom fashionable phrases become familiar just as their hollowness has been finally exposed.

But the impending stampede out of 'the growth of crime is an illusion' consensus should not obscure the lesson that for nearly thirty years it hindered British society from confronting a remark-able deterioration in its social environment, in comparison with which many of the problems that preoccupied the same consensus about the physical environment were remote in time and space and speculative in theory, but above all fashionable.

5

Influential Public Opinion and the Family Prior to 1960

From the middle of the nineteenth century until the late 1960s public opinion and individual action on family issues changed slowly, and the law was changed rarely. Marriage was a social institution. It was designed to guarantee, as far as possible, that each child was provided with two specific adults both of whom would be required to have an unqualified, full-time and long-term commitment to it. Each adult who chose to be sexually active was normally expected to form a household with only one sexual partner in the course of her or his lifetime, and never to have, and never to have had, anyone else as a sexual partner. This household was normally expected to be the 'home' of any children for the lifetime of their parents, even when the children themselves had created their own household as adults. Both adults brought to their children a lifetime complement of potential carers: grandparents, uncles, aunts, cousins and various 'in-laws'. Like crime, most of these arrangements for long escaped the attentions of the debunking intelligentsia. (There was always a good deal of debunking of the rule of premarital chastity. Debunking the rule of marital fidelity was much more rare and 'daring'.)

The Matrimonial Causes Act 1857 had allowed divorce through the courts on the basis only of the simple adultery of the wife, or the adultery of the husband if that was coupled with incest, bigamy, cruelty, two years' desertion, rape, or an unnatural offence. Lord Buckmaster's Act, 1923, made the husband's adultery alone sufficient grounds for the wife to obtain a divorce. The grounds were extended to such matters as desertion and incurable insanity in the Herbert Act in the mid-1930s.

It is often said that the low rates of divorce were due principally to the insuperable difficulties that confronted poor people in the legal system. But from 1878 the Magistrates' Court was enabled to grant separation orders and maintenance for the wife and children.

Almost a century has past since, in 1895, a wife could obtain a separation order on the grounds of her husband's conviction for assault on her, his desertion, his persistent cruelty, or his wilful neglect of maintenance. In 1902 habitual drunkenness was made an additional ground for separation. But women did not take advantage of these facilities to anything like the extent to which they took advantage of the roughly comparable facilities for divorce in the 1960s. During the years 1895-99 there was an annual average of only 600 applications for matrimonial orders, and in the following three quinquennia, up to the time of the Great War, the annual averages were 1,400, 2,200, and 2,200. During the inter-war period the rate was not only low by present-day standards, but also remarkably stable: the total for the five-years 1920-24 was 14,000, an annual average of 2,800, and the figures were the same in each of the five years period 1925-29 and 1930-34—a total of 14,000 in each quinquennium.[1]

The typical argument of the 1950s and 1960s was that the rising numbers of that period did not represent either a weakening of marriage as a publicly controlled institution or an increase in the instability of individual marriages. The increase in the divorce rates was simply a shift, actually beneficial to the health of marriage as a matter of public concern, as well as privately to the parties concerned, from 'informal to formalized marriage breakdown'.[2] With the increasing acceptance of legal divorce, fewer marriages were live-in divorces. The Morton Commission, reporting in 1956, was adamant that divorce should not simply provide a dignified and honourable means of release from a failed marriage.[3] As Rowntree wrote in 1964, the statistics of marriage and remarriage indicated a modern morality that was opposed to the idea of continuing with a marriage long since dead but it was certainly not a rejection of the institution of marriage.[4]

Even if it were to be accepted that the number of irretrievable marriage breakdowns had increased, this still did not indicate any decline in respect for the institution of marriage, or any decline in the quality of family life.

In 1963 Leo Abse's bill to allow divorce after seven years separation was unsuccessful in the Commons, but in the House of Lords the Archbishop of Canterbury announced the appointment of a Committee to investigate the principle of the breakdown of marriage.[5] The Group made the sharp distinction between the secular state's right to make marriage rules and the Church's right to have more stringent rules for its own adherents. The recognition of a secular divorce law, within the secular sphere, did not in itself compromise in any way its own doctrine. By 1971, however, the Archbishop's Group had rejected for the Church too the doctrine of the indissolubility of marriage.

For the state the question should be, the Group argued, did the evidence before the court reveal such failure in the matrimonial relationship that no reasonable probability remained of the spouses again living together for mutual comfort and support? That is, there was a definite shift in favour of the 'comfort'—to use that word again—of the adult parties.[6] But there was still no question of this being entirely their private concern; certainly there was no question that if there were children, the comfort of the parents was just as important an issue as the comfort of their children. The court must refuse to grant a decree if to grant it would be contrary to the public interest by its failing to protect—again—the *institution* of marriage. Furthermore, if it were not reasonably certain that the father after divorce would maintain his ex-wife and his children, the state should not release him from the marriage.[7]

In its report of 1966, *Reform of the Grounds For Divorce: The Field of Choice*, the Law Commission took as its basic assumption that a good divorce law should seek 'to buttress, rather than to undermine the stability of marriage'.[8] The existing law did not do all that it might 'to aid the stability of marriage', but tended rather to discourage attempts at reconciliation.[9] It was to the advantage of society, furthermore, to allow stable illicit unions where marriage was not possible because one of the partners was already married, but could not obtain a divorce, to be regularized through marriage.

Even into the early 1970s there was very little celebration of these changes as providing freedom from the obligations of institutionalized marriage, and from institutionalized parenthood within institutionalized marriage. The consensus continued to be, that the changes were intended to give, and in fact in general did give, life-long publicly-committed spousehood and long-term publicly-committed joint parenthood a new strength and prospect for success. The word 'family' was still generally taken to mean two mature adults' life-time commitment of their resources to one another and to their own children: material, sexual, practical and emotional. It did not mean that they would necessarily succeed in staying together permanently, much less staying together happily. It did mean that staying together permanently was their intention and their first priority. It also meant that they accepted the legitimacy of the social controls that condemned their behaviour if it threatened that permanency, and the rightness of their exercising the same social controls over others.

Actual families were adjudged better or worse as families, depending upon their success in realizing that state of affairs, with their own values and efforts, or under the blows or bounty of fate.

Just as crime rates had been low and constant through all the hardships and through all the vicissitudes of the first half of the century, including two major wars and one world slump, so had (to use the Mark Abrams' phrases) 'marrying habits' remained 'remarkably stable'.[10] G.D.H. Cole, for many years a prominent intellectual of the left, surveyed the scene in 1956 with typical complacency. The predominant type of social unit in Great Britain, he wrote, was the family, living together in a household that sometimes included other relatives, such as grandparents or other elderly persons, or brothers or sisters of the husband and wife. Family life had undergone large changes for the better. Quarrelling in the home had declined as a result of the improvement in housing standards. There had been a notable improvement in the care of children: they were markedly better fed and clothed and provided with opportunities for games than previous generations, and the proportion of neglected children had fallen.[11]

With the exception of a fringe of the bohemian (usually well-to-do) left, who obtained a certain frisson from their political and sexual eccentricity and notoriety, to be 'left' meant above all else extending family ideals of conduct, in this sense of family, into all the institutions and relationships of society.

Within the family, to be left was to insist that the lower standards of tenderness and fidelity required of men should be raised to those already required of women. For everyone in the family, the burdens and pleasures of the home, and the obligations and

35

opportunities that lay outside the home, were to be equalized and homogenized. The left, especially in its mainstream Labour form, welcomed and required a shift from paternalism to partnership. It advocated and applauded more rights for mothers and more duties for fathers. Where internal commitment to high standards of equal commitment was lacking then, at the very least, public contempt was a deserved and socially necessary sanction. Generally, the working-class family was held up not only as reformable, but even in its unreformed state as superior to the middle- and upper-class family, which was criticized for the subordination of the interests of the children to the selfish interest of the adults, and for the subordination of conjugal solidarity to the self-fulfilment of the individual spouses.[12]

6

Influential Public Opinion and the Family Since 1960

What part has the social-affairs intellectual played since the 1960s in the slackening of the detailed informal social controls (far more important than what happened to the broad and external legal framework), and in the attenuation of the internalized values that formerly attempted to tie the man by strict rules which governed, with more or less success in practice, sexual, conjugal and parental conduct?

There is today no general consensus on the family. This is most vividly demonstrable from the fact that there is no consensus on the meaning of the word itself. It has become largely a matter of group or even personal preference what public or private arrangements for the rearing of children, what arrangements for living together or not in the same household, what arrangements for mutual help and comfort, and what arrangements for the exchange of which sexual services, for what period, with what gender or by what technical arrangements for insemination, are 'family' arrangements.

British Social Attitudes 1986 showed that the general public was by then quite diverse in its opinion on marriage and divorce. Asked whether divorce should be made more difficult, large proportions of the population agreed that it should be made more difficult (40 per cent), disagreed (27 per cent), and would not commit themselves (33 per cent).

But 71 per cent of the general public still agreed with the proposition that 'as a society' we ought to do more to safeguard the 'institution' of marriage, with only 6 per cent disagreeing. An even higher proportion, 74 per cent, agreed that most people today take marriage too lightly.[1] A study published in 1993 of the opinion of 33-year-olds showed that nearly half of them believed that it was too easy to obtain a divorce nowadays. Fifteen per cent still thought that couples who had children should not separate.[2]

Public opinion in the 1980s and 1990s as expressed and led by members of the orthodox social-affairs intelligentsia, freed by their resources to exist in their second-hand worlds without disastrous consequences to themselves personally, was less favourable and more homogeneous than this general public opinion. They were much more likely to define the factual situation of the pre-1970s English family in its horrific reality as wife beating and the physical and sexual abuse of the child by the father, and therefore, of course, to morally condemn it as a social institution. The more quickly the number of children without fathers grew and the clearer the consequences of freeing men from their families became, the greater was the temptation of the advocates of 'alternative families' to justify themselves by painting the past of the two-parent family in ever darker colours of violence and child sexual abuse. The fall from grace of the male proletarian, from being the hero of the coming revolution, to bully, oppressor and incestuous sexual pervert, has been precipitous and quite remarkable.[3]

For example, using Robert Roberts' account of life in the slums of Salford, Lancashire (not in the extensive respectable working-class districts of the town) Peter Marris claims to show that 'fathers were petty tyrants, remote and harsh'.[4]

This seems to be independent of what Roberts actually wrote:

> One or two proletarian authors, writing about these times and of the slump between the wars ... by depicting its cruder and more moronic members ... end by caricaturing the class as a whole.[5]

Most men, even in the slum, Roberts says explicitly, were not boors and drunken braggarts.

> People *en masse*, it is true, had little education but the discerning of the time saw abundant evidence of intelligence, shrewdness, restraint and maturity. Of course, we had low 'characters' by the score, funny and revolting: so did every slum in Britain. Such types set no standards. In sobriety they knew their 'place' well enough. Very many families even in our 'low' district remained awesomely respectable over a lifetime. Despite poverty and appalling surroundings parents brought up their children to be decent, kindly, and honourable and often lived long enough to see them occupy a higher place socially than they had ever known themselves: the greatest satisfaction of all. It is such people and their children now who deny indignantly (and I believe rightly) that the slum life of the industrial North in this century, for all its horrors, was

ever so mindless and uncouth as superficial play or novel would have a later generation believe.[6]

The Edwardian slum child in Britain, Roberts writes, felt like his forebears an attachment to family life that a later age finds hard to understand.

> Home, however, poor, was the focus of all his love and interests ... songs about its beauties were ever on people's lips. 'Home Sweet Home', first heard in the 1870s, had become 'almost a second national anthem'. Few walls in lower-working-class houses lacked 'mottoes' ... attesting to domestic joys: EAST, WEST, HOME'S BEST; BLESS OUR HOME; GOD IS MASTER OF THIS HOUSE ... ; HOME IS THE NEST WHERE ALL IS BEST. To hear of a teen-ager leaving or being turned out of it struck dark fear in a child's mind. He could hardly imagine a fate more awful.[7]

A generation of more previously, Mearns had published one of the most famous and harrowing accounts of the life of the abject poor, *The Bitter Cry of Outcast London*. But he too is at pains to insist that even in the slums 'notwithstanding the sickening revelations of immorality [by which he means, mainly, prostitution] which have been disclosed to us, those who try to earn their bread by honest work far outnumber the dishonest. And it is to their infinite credit that it should be so, considering that they are daily face to face with the contrast between their wretched earnings and those which are the produce of sin.'[8]

These accounts of the slums are particularly interesting, because the accounts from contemporary social researchers of working-class family life outside the slums, the family life of the respectable working class, was extremely favourable to it (as we show in our *English Ethical Socialism*).[9]

Working-class mothers come out of modern descriptions and moral evaluations of the pre-1960s' family somewhat better. It is acknowledged that they were heroic in the struggles against the adversities of their physical and conjugal conditions. Again, in reviewing Roberts' book, Marris characterizes the mother as 'slaving obediently', struggling to hold the family above social disgrace. On the positive side, he says, there was courage in this striving for respectability. But the overall judgement is negative, for respectability was itself merely 'implicit social subservience'—a very common theme and condemnation from the orthodox social-affairs intelligentsia, and most popular among those with no proletarian background whatsoever.

We find with the family what we found with everyday civility: a consensus that is contradicted by such statistics as exist. If we agree to discard the statistics as useless, we have the literature and other artifacts of contemporaneous intellectuals. If we discard those as the tainted products of the 'hired prize-fighters of the bourgeoisie', as Marx called John Stuart Mill, then we are left with the memories of people who lived at the time in the families and neighbourhoods of the time.

On what grounds do the orthodox social-affairs intellectuals, very many of them not having lived at that time, and even more of them not having lived in those neighbourhoods, prefer their own version of those people's lives to the version that those people have of their own? How do they account for the wide-spread and long-lasting appeal among ordinary working people, up to the 1960s, of 'Home Sweet Home'? How do they account for the widespread and long-lasting appeal among ordinary people, up to the 1960s, of Felicia Hemans' verses:

> The merry homes of England—
> Around their hearths at night,
> What gladsome looks of household love
> Meet in the ruddy light!
> There woman's voice flows forth in song,
> Or childhood's tale is told;
> Or lips move tunefully along
> Some glorious page of old.
>
> The free fair homes of England,
> Long, long, in hut and hall,
> May hearts of native proof be reared
> To guard each hallowed wall.
> And green for ever be the groves,
> And bright the flowery sod,
> Where first the child's glad spirit loves
> Its country and its God.

It is readily conceded, of course, that Hemans' verses do not describe all families throughout their whole existence. The groves, admittedly, were now in the local municipal park, and the flowery sod down at Dad's allotment. Those who remembered, recited and heard these verses knew all that quite well. Were the people who formed opinion in those days in those neighbourhoods, when very few men, and even fewer women from working-class homes went into higher education, so much less intelligent and able than the average orthodox intellectual today?

How do they account for the popularity in working-class homes in County Durham and Northumberland, over a period of half-a-century, of the print showing the young pitman in his neat cottage, with the clippy mat on the spotless brick floor, tenderly if gingerly holding the baby, 'Aa wish yor muther wad cum'?[10] How do they account for the even greater popularity of the song, 'Cum, Geordie, haad the Bairn'? A father's gentleness with the baby is what counts, Geordie says. 'It's nee use gettin' vexed/It winnet please the bairn,/Or ease a mind perplext.'[11]

Jack Lawson provides a first-hand account of how he, a young miner, did get to Oxford in 1906.[12] He also gives vivid first-hand accounts of family life at the end of the nineteenth century and into the early 1930s in Boldon Colliery, a mining town in County Durham. 'As I write I hear my neighbour return from his day's work in the mine. Quiet, strong, a good workman, a good father, a good husband. From home to pit, from pit to home. His luxury is his home. He loves and is loved ... A brave, good man who is not aware of it. ... Not economic theory, but ... calloused hands, is the most challenging fact in the world's life today.' He dedicated the book 'to my fellow miners'. Did he dedicate it to his neighbours and work-mates who he must have known to be uncouth bullies and sexual perverts in their families, if they were?[13]

Robin Humphrey has studied family life during the inter-war, wartime and early post-war period in Ferryhill, also in Co. Durham, a town in the heart of the coal-mining district. Dr. Humphrey painstakingly collected verbatim accounts from the people concerned—the people still living who had experienced it (and were still benefiting from what remained of it). What impressed him above all was the sheer strength—though if it were to survive, the restrictiveness—of the kinship unit and the emotional and material support it gave to its members.[14]

In Dr. Humphrey's view, not crime, but the miners' family, and all the working-class institutions of the Cooperative store, the working-men's club, the football teams and cycling clubs were forced on Ferryhill by the poverty, unemployment and poor housing of the time.

Were ordinary people wrong in supposing that these descriptions and sentiments corresponded in some important way with their own experience and ideals? Is the speculative and *post factum* version of commonplace and culturally permitted or overlooked brutality and perversion of husbands and fathers, preferred by today's conforming intellectuals, right? Why should anybody think so?

Descartes, in the opening passage of his *Discourse on Method*, speaks of the great blessing bestowed on the whole of humankind, good sense. He is filled with admiration on his travels by the sight of people in all walks of life who are masters of their own near business.[15] He was keenly aware of the dangers of contradicting common sense, and the importance, when one does so, of not being too rash in the certainty that something better is being put in its place.

> The greatest minds, as they are capable of the highest excellences, are open likewise to the greatest aberrations; and those who travel very slowly may yet make far greater progress, provided that they always keep to the straight road, than those who, while they run, forsake it.[16]

He never experienced the kind of world we live in, where nearly everyone takes a more or less inattentive interest in remote affairs. Most take an interest in the social policies of the government of the UK and the affairs of state of foreign powers, as the ordinary reader of *The Guardian* or ordinary viewer of News At Ten forms her or his opinion of American policy in Mogadishu; the extent of homelessness in London and the reasons for it; the justification for riots on Tyneside; whether or not Wearmouth colliery should be closed; or the plight or otherwise of single mums in West India House in Stepney. Nobody is gifted in these matters with the common sense that comes from the repeated, near, and consequential experiences of small communities of people.[17]

Except for the occasional public outcry (and representative democracy is important partly because public outcries can occur and can affect events) the consequences of forming opinions about something one knows little about, that is, forming opinions outside the scope of common sense, are in the individual case trifling, though cumulatively they become decisive as 'public opinion'. The errors of individuals taking their interest in great affairs from the armchair generally speaking have no consequences.

But when *de haut en bas* people with power and influence take it upon themselves to overturn the common sense of those subject to their power, they do well to be modest about their own superior knowledge. When working-class areas were cleared in the 1960s by the central government and local authorities, the consequences did not fall on the planners and architects. If they had, their own common sense, the knowledge and interpretation of their own immediate experience, would have tempered their confident contempt for the common sense of the residents in the localities affected.[18]

The working-class people to whom Hemans' verses and Hedley's images strongly appealed did not in those days go to university. They had not been awarded certificates that proved that they were qualified to speak with authority on these matters. They had few experts legitimated by being at the head of their pressure groups, and therefore listed to be invited by the gate-keepers of the media of mass communication to persuade the remote general public of the rectitude of their clients' interpretation of their own position. But were they really as gullible as the doctrine of false consciousness implies, that they could be told *and believe*, decade after decade, generation after generation, blatant lies, not about the German national character; not about the factional struggles of the Spanish Civil War; not about claims for the technical differences between two equally good toothpastes; not about Heaven and Hell; not about dialectical materialism as applied to the crisis of capitalism; not about whether the earth was spherical or flat, but about their own home and neighbourhood life?

Cobbett was the spokesman for the working class in the first decades of the nineteenth century. He, too, remarked on people's good sense in matters that were part and parcel of their own immediate experience. Losing his way in Wiltshire one Friday he came to the village of Tangley, where he conversed with an astute

mother of about thirty years of age who, as far as he could tell, had not been further than two-and-a-half miles from her birthplace in her entire life. 'It is a great error to suppose that people are rendered stupid by always remaining in the same place.'[19] Of course today she might well have become a university professor.

The current consensus of the progressive intelligentsia on the consequences of the privatization of marriage and the disappearance of sociological fatherhood is fairly represented by the content of a speech by Neil Kinnock, at that time Leader of the Labour Party, to the 1990 social services annual conference. It was welcomed by the secretary of the Association of Directors of Social Services as providing a 'cohesive and non-stigmatizing' range of family policies.

Kinnock said that births outside marriage and single parenthood meant only that the family was changing, not collapsing. Those who tried to represent these 'non-traditional' families as evidence of social delinquency, a delinquency that had to be combatted by sanctions, had 'no intentions that could be described as good'.

This is the message of advisers who had made their way within the student movement in the 1970s. Whatever their own standards, they must have responded to and been affected by the pastime and political preoccupations of their temporarily rootless constituents. They now move within the pressure-group milieux of the capital; and to an unusual extent among people employed in the media whose income and employment conditions enable them to manage quite well as lone parents. Even today, however, the commonest attitude of potential Labour voters over the age of thirty in a Labour heartland like Sunderland, chewing over the latest outrage by young men on their housing estate, is not theirs. It is not that the non-traditional family is a viable and even admirable alternative. It is rather, 'I've got nothing but sympathy for the bairns. And it's hard lines when a lad can't say, "That's my Dad!", and be proud of it'. How many times have I heard variations on that theme? Did Mr Kinnock's advisers persuade him that Labour would help itself to be returned to power by being identified in the public mind as the party of the non-traditional family?

But he shared the consensus of confusion. For, as he also said in the same speech, there had been a corrosion of family values—presumably the values that required the permanent commitment of the father. This corrosion was 'destructive of the family'. The destruction of the family was 'harmful to society'.

This harm to society and corrosion of family values was due, however, to government policy, which had resulted in a housing shortage, youth unemployment, debt, and poverty. How severe the housing shortage, the unemployment and the poverty of the 1980s and 1990s were as compared with the times that preceded the corrosion of family values, Mr. Kinnock did not say.[20]

In the course of twenty years the opinion-formers who had come to dominate the Labour Party on family matters had indeed brought it by a strange route to a fateful destination.

Not Deteriorating Only Changing

The 'not deteriorating, only changing' thesis was still widely disseminated its pure form by social-affairs intellectuals in 1993.

The Guardian published a typical article by Malcolm Dean.[1] It was an attack on A.H. Halsey's statement that, in supplying its children with material resources, affection and supervision, the lone-parent family was necessarily on the average less effective than the family with a father who had publicly and internally committed himself to staying with his wife and children, and who succeeded in doing so; and that, almost without exception, research studies confirmed this.[2]

It is important to recognize that the lone-parent category is not a scientific, but a propaganda one. For propaganda, but not for scientific purposes, it is useful to obscure the differences between the situation and consequences of having had a committed father who has died, on the one hand, and on the other the situation and consequences of, for example, having had a father who did not marry the mother before the child was born and has never been present in the child's life. The good results from the children of the widow then bolster the results from the children of the never-present father.

Even more importantly for propaganda purposes: so long as they are included without differentiation in the same category of lone parent, the public sympathy and willing support for the widow, found in all societies, can be shared by the woman who has no 'sociological' father for her child, who in most societies (Malinowski says in all societies) is the object of public disapproval and grudging support. Of societies studied by anthropologists it is frequently reported that the sociological father is not the biological father but, for example, a mother's brother. But all children have a sociological father and all boys are brought up to effectively discharge the obligations, whatever they are in his society, of fatherhood.

Malcolm Dean began, promisingly, by specifying that he was dealing with one sub-group of lone-parent children, those 'living with lone mothers who had never married'. These did 'as well as' and 'some slightly better than' children in two-parent families. But in the body of the article, having carefully designated the category to which his statement applies, he argues as though he had not limited himself to this category, and for much of the article he talks as though there were equal or superior benefits for a child from being brought up in a lone-parent family in general as compared with the child from the two-parent family. If it were true (it is *not* true) that illegitimate father-absent children did do better than legitimate children with their fathers in two-parent families, then there would be some undisclosed logic in his argument, for illegitimate father-absent children do worse than other groups of lone-parent children (that *is* true). If the worst sub-group of the lone-parent children did better than the total group of two-parent children, the remaining sub-groups of lone-parent children must have done even better against the total group of two-parent children.

If Malcolm Dean, at the other extreme, was saying no more than that *some* of the children in the group of illegitimate father-absent children did as well as, and some better than, *some* of the children in the group whose parents were married and were together raising their legitimate child, there would have been no basis for disagreement between Malcolm Dean and Professor Halsey. Professor Halsey fully recognized and was at pains to make clear on all occasions that he was talking about frequency distributions. The set of children from one domestic situation do well *with greater frequency* than the set of children from other domestic situations. But in fact Malcolm Dean has gone far beyond this. His having written the article only makes sense on the assumption that he is of the 'not deteriorating, only changing' school of thought: one group average is the same as the other group average; in fact, what Professor Halsey maintains is the better group, is in some respects, Malcolm Dean states, the inferior group.

It may be that the *certainty* that there are *some* children from lone-parent families who do as well as, and some better than *some* children from two-parent families is the initial truth that sets

Malcolm Dean on his train of error in 'proving' to his satisfaction, and to the satisfaction of the conforming social-affairs intellectual, that there is nothing to choose between lone-parent families and families with two married parents as social structures for raising children.

Quite senior academics with a special interest in the field are prone to make exactly the same elementary mistake. They have directed me to studies which they said showed that the life chances of the child in some alternative domestic arrangement or another (lone parents, lesbian couples, males homosexual couples etc.) were not inferior in any or in some respects to those of the child brought up in the family of two married parents bringing up their own legitimate child. All that they showed was the usual, totally familiar and almost inevitable thing, that there was an overlap between the two distributions. The better end of the worse distribution did better than the worse end of the better distribution.

For evidence, Malcolm Dean cited the work of an important researcher in the field. What did Elsa Ferri actually say? Certainly, for *all* 'children living with lone parents' she said exactly the opposite to what Malcolm Dean attributes to her. She said that 'in every area investigated', those in one-parent families were found to be 'disadvantaged when compared with their counterparts in two-parent homes'.[3]

Her research was based on a nationally representative sample of children from lone-parent families, derived from two studies. One was of 11-year-olds from the National Child Development Study (NCDS) of 17,000 children born in Great Britain in one week in March 1958. 748 of these 11-year-olds were being brought up by a lone parent. 652 of the children were in lone-mother situations: 58 of them (9 per cent) because of their illegitimacy.[4] The other was a special study of a sub-sample of the lone-parent families in the NCDS when the children were aged 15.

The three main problems confronting lone-parent families, she wrote, were income, housing, and the related issues of employment and day care.

Children in one-parent families are likely to go through childhood deprived of many of the essentials and luxuries which are taken for granted in our affluent society; a situation likely to create frustration and resentment in the children themselves and in the parents who are unable to provide what other [i.e. two-parent] families give their children.[5]

Children in father-absent families were eight times more likely to be in receipt of free school meals than children in two-parent families. Children in all lone-parent situations (they were mainly father-absent situations) were more likely to be living in the 'vulnerable privately-rented sector', to have poorer quality accommodation in terms of the availability of basic amenities, to be sharing their beds at the age of 11, to have moved home more frequently, and to have changed school more frequently. 'Such findings are particularly disturbing in the light of research evidence which has shown the relationship between adverse housing conditions and poor educational and social development.'[6]

Meeting 'the need for adequate supervision before and after school' was another 'major problem' facing lone parents who went out to work. During the holidays one third of the father-only and one half of the father-absent children were 'left to fend for themselves'.[7]

Where lone parenthood was the result of the breakdown of the marriage, 40 per cent of the parents said that the children's behaviour had been affected at the time, and 25 per cent said that their were still current behaviour problems attributable to the family situation. Two main reactions were reported. One was withdrawal, anxiety, and depression, sometimes with physical symptoms which resulted in frequent absence from school. The other—especially among the 15-year-olds—was aggression, hostility, and resistance to control. 'The isolation of these parents and the burden of total responsibility which they carried seems to have made them highly self-critical and anxious, and perhaps over-ready to perceive problems in their children, which they saw as the result of their family situation.'

The parent is under stress due to having to cope alone. One of the main points to emerge, she writes, was the great emotional difficulty the lone parent had experienced in trying to be both mother and father to the children. 'Many parents, but especially the mothers, talked about the problems of being the only source of both authority and affection.' Other mothers were worried about the effect upon their sons' development of the lack of an adult male

49

in the family, and were conscious of their own inability to share in their sons' interests. The lone fathers were more likely to mention difficulties in offering the children the comfort and emotional support which had previously been provided by the mother.[8]

We now turn to Malcolm Dean's specific category of the children whose fathers had made them illegitimate and were not part of the home in which they were being brought up—those with never-married lone mothers. Had these children escaped the disadvantages of other lone-parent children? Did these children do as well as and in some cases better than two-parent children? *Had* Ferri come up with the highly unusual and counter-intuitive finding that as a category the 'children living with lone mothers who had never married', of all unlikely children, had done 'as well as' and some 'slightly better than' children in two-parent families, when the lone-parent child in general did worse?

It is just plausible that with the cultural changes beginning to stir specifically round about 1958, the still small group of never-married mothers could have been predominantly drawn from the rich and the well-educated, and that would explain how in the Ferri study they did as well as all classes and all educational levels among the two-parent families—if that is what she had found and reported.

But Ferri found nothing of the sort. The nearest we get in her study to 'mothers who were never married' are the mothers of 11-year-olds who were 'without a father because of their illegitimacy'. They were neither from the higher social classes nor from the best educated strata. They were drawn predominantly from the semi-skilled and unskilled, and from among the most poorly educated of women.

Ferri shows that, far from 'doing as well as, and some slightly better than' the two-parent families, these fatherless illegitimate children brought up by their mothers alone not only did worse as a whole group than two-parent families as a whole group, they generally did worse than children in all other lone-parent situations, not to speak of two-parent situations. In lone-parent households, on the average disadvantaging their children as compared with the traditional family, the children brought up by widowed mothers did best (and there are indeed good grounds for including the widow in the traditional, and not with the lone-parent category). The children of the divorced or separated lay in between, as we would expect from a very diverse group.

On poverty, for example, Ferri states that the proportion of lone-parent children taking free school meals was 'particularly high where the children were without a father due to illegitimacy'. On social adjustment: the mean score of boys whose mothers were alone because the child was illegitimate was 14 (a high score on the Bristol Social Adjustment Guide indicated maladjustment); for boys whose mothers were alone because of marital breakdown it was 13; for boys from two-parent families 9.4; and for boys whose mothers were alone because of widowhood 9.[9]

But she did find in a tiny group a tiny anomaly. It is this tiny group and tiny anomaly that—quite characteristically—enter the canon of the 'not deteriorating, only changing' school of thought as part of its exiguous and egregious evidence.

Out of the 58 illegitimate children who were in a father-absent domestic situation, 26 of them had mothers who had been in full-time work at some time in the previous year.

It was this very small groups of 26 children that threw up the curious quirk in the study which formed the basis of *The Guardian's* proof that the lone mother who had never married did as well as, or even better than, two permanently married parents. And they did so on only one measure: these 26 children turned out to have higher reading scores than the children from two-parent manual social-class families.[10]

This was a most unusual finding. Here was a group which was heavily skewed towards low social class, poor housing, income at social security levels, and with the only available parent out of the house in full-time work—and these children, contrary to all statistical expectations, did best of all in the reading test.

Were reading skills of the fatherless illegitimate 11-year-olds helped, perhaps, by the fact that, even though the whole group of the mothers of the illegitimate fatherless was drawn disproportionately from the unskilled and semi-skilled, the mothers who worked full-time in this group were disproportionately from the highest social classes?

We are not given the social-class breakdown for this sub-set (even though we are given at any rate some social-class breakdown of all other sub-sets). But we are informed that the total of the never-marrieds who were from Registrar General's (RG) highest social class, class I, was zero, and there was only one from RG class II—and indeed only a further five from RG non-manual class III (of those for whom a social-class designation was made).[11] There was not therefore a lot of scope for high-class full-time working mothers to make their contribution to the high average reading scores of the group of 26 as a whole.

If the success at reading were a statistically significant finding that could indeed be generalized to all the children of never-married mothers who went out to full-time work, there would remain two other possible explanations.

The first depends upon the fact that the whole group of never-marrieds is heavily weighted by the favourable reading factor of 'only one child in the family'. Not only does the whole group benefit in its reading skills from this; it is likely that the full-time working mothers came disproportionately from the smaller families. The production of only-child families seems to be physically, socially and psychologically more likely in the lone-parent situation. In so far as this benefits the child by improving his chances at school, that must stand to the credit of this type of family structure. It is good at producing this state of affairs, just as it is as a structural form relatively poor at producing emotional support for the mother, steady and durable affection for the child, and freedom from stresses contingent upon relative poverty.

The second remaining explanation would be that all or nearly all the children had enjoyed the 'head start' of state nurseries. In order to show that lone parents did as well as two parents it would have to be shown, then, that the lone-parent children with a nursery education did as well as two-parent children with a nursery education—not just that lone-parent children with a nursery education did as well as all two-parent children, whether the two-parent children had been to a nursery or not.

Let us suppose that state nursery education for these children of these unmarried mothers does help account for their pre-eminence in reading skills as against the combined nursery and non-nursery children in all other groups.

That would not show that this is true of their vastly more numerous equivalents today. Nurseries in which the children of lone mothers were the exception are likely to be different environments for the unmarried lone mother's child from nurseries where they are form a sizeable minority or even a substantial majority.

The state may be endlessly willing to make up, non-judgementally, a child's deficiencies in money, affection, security and (still to some extent) honour. But as the supply of children with disadvantages increases, and the supply of children without disadvantages to provide a benign environment for them diminishes, the task of the nursery school necessarily becomes one of ever-mounting difficulty. As the Economic and Social Research Council reported in Autumn 1993, public nurseries were by then reserved 'almost exclusively' for children from households 'with *acute* or *multiple* problems'.[12]

Public opinion in the abstract broadly shares the view, of course, that more should be done for the blameless child of the never-present father by providing it among other things with nursery education. In that regard the position is little changed from the late 1950s and early 1960s, when unmarried lone parents were a small minority of the population, and were regarded by themselves as well as others as presenting problems that the majority without those problems should help to solve by state welfare provisions. With the growth in the numbers and proportion of children from father-absent families political deeds have contradicted charitable sentiments. For the past 14 years the electorate has failed to vote Labour into government. This indicates that its willingness to make up the shortfall in resources for the child of money, supervision and affection in the household headed by an ever-increasing number of never-married lone-mothers has not grown proportionately to the need.

It does seem a slow business to overcome the prejudice that if a person puts himself or herself into a position of disadvantage as a result of attractive short-term behaviour that others prudently avoid, that the prudent people should not have to bear the costs. Burke put the point of view of these prejudiced people in these words: 'the retrograde order of society has something flattering to the dispositions of mankind. The life of adventurers, gamesters, gipsies, beggars and robbers is not unpleasant. It requires restraint to keep men from falling into that habit'. Order, frugality and industry, and the slow and steady progress of unvaried occupation, with the prospect only of a limited mediocrity at the end of long labour are by comparison with the life of fornication free from family responsibilities 'to the last degree tame, languid and insipid'. Why should they use the resources derived from their self-denial to ameliorate the hardships that are the result of self-indulgence?[13] However much we may be shocked by that, it is the way some people do still think. Some of them are even prepared to harden their hearts against the children and continue to use the parable prohibited by Ezekiel: 'The fathers have eaten sour grapes, and the children's teeth are set on edge'.[14]

But it is far the most likely that none of the above explanations for the good reading scores of these 26 children is necessary. For it is in all probability an anomaly resulting from the small numbers involved. Some of the children in this very small group just happened to be exceptionally good readers, something that is bound to happen by chance sooner or later in any field of statistical study.

It this type of single finding, in this case the reading-test results of these 26 11-year-olds whose fathers had not married their mothers, who were being brought up without a father, and whose mothers had been in full-time work in the year previous to the study, which have been used to bolster the proposition that lone-parent families in general do just as well, and in some cases better than two-parent families in general. This general proposition has then been solemnly accepted by serious opinion, and proclaimed in the broadsheet press and in discussion programmes on radio and television.

Yet it is difficult to find any study at all that shows that the families in the whole category of lone parents produce results for their children that are as good as those of the whole category of two parents. It is even more difficult to find one that shows them producing average results that are as good as families in a publicly defined and controlled relationship of permanent commitment; or that in otherwise similar circumstances of amount or source of income, housing conditions, social class, access to and use of outside assistance (or whatever an interlocutor would want to specify) the lone-parent children do as well.

8

The Weakness of the Case for the Consensus

A similar typical generalization on the basis of a deeply defective understanding of the research material could be seen in the *Observer*, another important newspaper of enlightened opinion.

The *Observer* published an article by a producer of BBC programmes on social affairs, which characteristically argued that lone parenting was not inferior to the parenting which included parenting by a successfully committed father.[1] This article, again characteristically, gave what were purported to be the conclusions on lone parenting of another important researcher in this field, in this case Eileen Crellin, who was quoted verbatim:

> One would expect a lower incidence of maladjustment among children who had since birth lived with both their natural parents since this is akin to the most typical family constellation in the population as a whole; or one might argue that the child in the one-parent family would be more likely to show maladjusted behaviour than one from a two-parent family, even if only one was his natural parent.

However, surprisingly, this proved not to be the case. Little difference was found between those living with their natural parents, those growing up in some other type of two-parent family and those being brought up by their mother only. Indeed, there was a lower proportion of maladjusted children living alone with their mothers.[2]

That this statement, as 'Crellin's conclusions on the role of single-parenthood', went unchallenged through all editorial processes is another common example in this field of sociological scotoma, the failure to perceive errors when they confirm the intellectual consensus. It illustrates once again the carelessness, if not recklessness, in the handling of arguments that depend upon the facts of the case, of an intelligentsia deeply but now unconsciously contaminated by the anti-positivism discussed above.

Crellin is presented as saying that in general being brought up in lone-parent family actually leads to less maladjustment among children than being brought up in a two-parent family. That is an amazing proposition to anyone not determined to believe it. To check whether this is what Crellin did indeed say, and to conclusively refute it, was the task of a few minutes study of the easily available text by any ordinary person at his or her local library. It was not beyond the resources, and was certainly well within the duties, of a major world newspaper.

For Crellin in the passage quoted is not in any way or to the slightest degree giving her general 'conclusions on the role of single parenting'. She is drawing attention to the *peculiarities*, the exceptional nature, of her *small illegitimate sub-group*, composed mainly of father-absent families. She shows that it does worse across the board than the legitimate group, composed mainly of two-parent families. Within the sub-group of the illegitimate children, the children in father-absent situations did better than the children living in a situation where their 'illegitimate' father was present with their 'illegitimate' mother. By no stretch of the imagination did they as a category do as well as or in some cases better than the children in families in which both parents were married when the child was born, and were bringing up the child together.[3] All that she found was that the *seriously disadvantaged* lone-mother illegitimate children did somewhat better than the *seriously disadvantaged* two-natural-parent illegitimate children—those whose natural, illegitimate, father had stayed in the household.

She offered a possible explanation for this: the illegitimate children are so severely disadvantaged in so many ways already that the domestic structure they end up in then makes relatively little difference to them.[4]

One could be hardly farther away from the proposition that Crellin concludes that the single parent in general does better than two parents in general.

One of the exceptional journalists who did not accept at face value the pronouncements and prejudices of conforming academics was Melanie Phillips. She published an account of a seminar she had attended in 1991. The Editor has already referred to it in the Foreword. At the seminar a social scientist 'of the left' had, she wrote, 'fiercely denounced' the view that children from broken or never-constituted families were disadvantaged.

57

She telephoned him afterwards to ask about the research on which he based his assertions. 'The social scientist proved surprisingly reluctant to answer the question.' He released a stream of 'emotional invective', calling into question the mental faculties of those who had put forward the view with which he disagreed. Melanie Phillips says that she then pressed him repeatedly to identify the research findings upon which he depended.

His final reply, as summarized by Melanie Phillips, was anti-positivism at its clearest. 'Of course it was correct *as far as the research was concerned*', he said, that children brought up by both their married parents did better on the average than other children. 'But where did that get anyone? Nowhere!' Only research that is convenient for advocacy can be permissibly publicized: 'Why were they so concerned about the rights of the child? What of the rights of the parents, which were just as important?'[5]

A British Home Office study by Riley and Shaw is frequently referred to by subscribers to the 'not deteriorating' consensus.[6] It at least has the merit that it is one of the rare examples which does make the clear and outright claim, in context, not indeed that the lone-parent structure is superior, but that it not inferior in preventing teenage delinquency.

But the briefest glance at it shows that it provides them with a very insecure refuge. Riley and Shaw state that when 378 boys were asked if they had committed any one of 21 offences in the previous year, ranging from breaking a bottle in the street to arson and burglary, the prevalence of delinquency so defined was not higher among teenagers from one-parent households.

Using this definition, they find that crime correlates with very few things at all. This immediately raises the very pertinent question of whether the failure to reveal differences is merely an artifact of a measure that is intrinsically a poor discriminator.

Even so, they report that boys who said they were closer to their mothers than their fathers or equally close to both were almost three times more likely to be delinquent than those who were closer to their fathers.[7] To an unbiased person this would strongly suggest the hypothesis for investigation that fathers are effective in keeping their sons away from crime. Riley and Shaw do not say whether they include lone-parent families here or not.[8] (Lone-parent families are nearly all lone-mother families.) Given that a preference for the mother emerged as such a strong criminogenic factor on their definition of crime, one would have expected that lone-mother families, more than any other, would contain children who preferred their mothers to their fathers.

The same point applies here as was made in the previous chapter. It is the easiest thing in the world to show, absolutely correctly, that many children from almost any given family arrangement do better than many of the children from almost any other family arrangement. Displaying good cases from the worse distribution and the bad cases from the better distribution makes for an easily-grasped and dramatic newspaper feature or television or radio programme—or even academic conference paper when presented to a compliant audience. Making a case about statistical distributions and averages is not only confusing and dull, but actually is not capable of being accommodated within the time and space constraints of journalism. So it often looks as if contention that 'one form of arrangement for the upbringing of the child is as good as any other for the child' has been confirmed, when all that has been demonstrated is that the distributions overlap.

If the average child from the average lone-parent situation is indeed doing as well as the average child from the family where the legitimate, successfully committed natural father has brought it up with the successfully committed natural mother, what is the problem we are being called upon to solve?

This implication of the 'not-deteriorating-only-changing' view embarrasses only some orthodox social-affairs intellectuals. Others confidently do identify the problem. The problem for them is the people who say that there is a problem. Their premise is that all family situations are roughly similar in their proportionate production of good and bad results. There is nothing defective in bringing up a child in a lone-parent situation that is not more or less exactly balanced by the defects of other arrangements for bringing up a child.

The more uncompromising version is that the only disadvantage that impacts on the child is that it suffers from bearing the label 'problem child'. It bears the unpleasant burden of being stigmatized. There are no other consequences, including no adverse consequences from being inappropriately labelled. That is why (on the contention of this school of thought) no discernible differences appear between the average performance of children brought up in lone-parent situations as compared with two-parent families.

The less uncompromising version is that there are differences in performance, but the sole cause for these differences is stigma. It is *saying* that lone-parent families are problematical, and only that, that makes them so. This point of view, or rather (characteristically) an inconsistent muddle of the two, has no difficulty in passing muster for publication in another of the major organs of well-informed opinion, *The Independent*. The two major assumptions of the article are that politicians and sociologists have been unremittingly critical of the father-absent situation, and that factually there is no basis for the criticism. 'Single parents carry the blame for a range of ills caused by a hypocritical and merciless society.' The article begins with a blunt accusation against the people who report that research in this country on the life chances of children show father-absent children to be disadvantaged, especially where the father did not marry the mother. They are lying; and they are sly liars, or insidious liars. 'I will *never* accept the weaselly mendacity of the image created by sociologists.' She then goes on to attack only Professor A.H. Halsey, one of the few sociologists who have discussed these findings in recent years.

> Take this headline from *The Times* last week: 'The children of lone parents *tend to* do badly at school, suffer more illnesses and *are likely to* die earlier, according to *some* sociologists'.
>
> There is a really killer paragraph in the article: the very thing to break the confidence of an exhausted young woman ...
>
> Does he stigmatise the off-spring of politicians, diplomats, lawyers or doctors? Yet he would find a lot of 'tend-tos' among that lot, and some very 'unstable parenting'. I was once told by the wife of a house-master at Eton that she never came across so many emotionally starved boys.
>
> ... Were children whose fathers died during the war, leaving widowed mothers to bring them up, called 'deprived' or deemed likely to die earlier? Certainly not. ...
>
> Why are today's 2 million children from a home with only one parent deemed to be inherently unfortunate? Is not their misfortune created by politicians and society, which ... utter dire predictions about their future health, happiness and success? Do not these become self-fulfilling, just *because* they are so widely touted?

What are mothers supposed to do? ... Is the subtext that if they had kept their knees together, none of this would have happened?[9]

The article is accompanied by a prominent picture of what is probably a stern Victorian father casting his daughter and bastard grandchild into the street. Standards were so strict and different at that time that Dickens actually pictures the *father* of his erring daughter, Oliver Twist's mother, 'goaded by shame and dishonour' fleeing with his other children 'into a remote part of Wales, changing his very name, that his friends would not know of his retreat; and here, no great while afterwards, he was found dead in his bed'.[10] Equating Professor Halsey's work with early- or mid-Victorian attitudes to and treatment of the fatherless child is as nice an example as one could wish to find of the mind-set of the current conformist. It dismisses what is 'crudely' true, such as research findings on father-absent children, and expresses what is 'really' true, in this case the truth that any statements about the superiority of the family of the married pair, however well disguised and indeed impregnable as academic discourse, are really the satanic verses of people who seek only to do the lone mother and her helpless baby harm.

9

Families Without Grandfatherhood

One line of argument which is used to attempt to save the 'not-deteriorating-only-changing' consensus is as familiar as it is specious. It is not denied, in this approach, that the lone parent is less well-resourced with money, potential affection-givers and potential supervisors. Nor is it denied that these defects are deleterious for the child's bodily safety, education, law-abidingness, and so forth.

But all these things, it is said, can be notionally detached from fact of the absence of the husband and father. The conclusion is, then, that it is not lone parenthood 'as such' that constitutes the problem, but only the things that are associated with lone parenthood.

'Children who experience poverty where the successfully committed father and the successfully committed mother are both present suffer as much from that poverty as children in father-absent families.' Therefore, the argument runs, it is not the absence of the father as such, but poverty that is the problem. In other realms of discourse, less driven by ideology, this would be immediately recognized as a *non sequitur*. For lone-parent families as a group, because they are lone-parent families, are much more likely to be poor, and statistically are much poorer on the average, than the families with two successfully committed parents as a group. They therefore produce a higher proportion of children suffering from poverty, if poverty is defined as being in the lowest income group.

Even on the material level (where in principle it is far easier for deficiencies to be made up by fellow-citizens) unless and until fellow-citizens do become willing to remove all or most of the material disadvantages which necessarily stem from the fact that there is only one breadwinner instead of potentially two, then the figures will continue to show father-absent children suffering the disadvantages of poverty. On the average the lone parent is not able to provide a total situation which is relatively free from the stresses that arise from low or unreliable income.

Susie Orbach, writing in *The Guardian*, maintained that father-absence forces us to recognize the 'independence, capability and power' of women. That many women are unavoidably lone parents and that the fault lies entirely with the man is not doubted. Nor is it doubted that many of them are competent, that many of them by their competence overcome the handicaps of their position, and many of them do so by heroic self-sacrifice. But most of them are only showing independence within a framework of dependence on strangers. The means of life of the majority of father-absent families are not generated by their own efforts. They are generated by their fellow-citizens. The Department of Social Security (DSS) research report on the subject in 1991 showed that 73 per cent of lone mothers depended on income support at the time of the survey, and of these only 28 per cent had been in regular full-time employment before they had their child and the father-absent situation was created.[1]

Because of the situation in which they find themselves, both the teenage mother and her fatherless child suffer material disadvantages.[2] The teenage unmarried mother is more likely than her peers to languish in the lowest income group. The DSS report showed that nine out ten of all unmarried lone parents were on income support.[3] Income support provides a low income compared with that from employment either with or without maintenance.[4] The average income of father-absent lone-parent families was the lowest of all categories of lone parent.[5] But a 16-18 year-old receives a lower rate of state benefit even than older unmarried lone mothers —and an unmarried mother under the age of 16 is not entitled to any Income Support for herself or her children.[6] The mother and child are more likely than their peers to face housing difficulties.[7] The child itself is more likely to die and less likely to be well-formed.[8]

The same argument is used across the board. 'Babies and infants who suffer from lack of supervision in two-parent families are just as likely to suffer the consequences as children who suffer from lack of supervision in lone-parent families.' Of course. But lone-parents, because they are lone-parents, have fewer resources for supervision, on the average, than two-parent families. In their study, Judge and Benzeval showed that the children from father-absent families had 'the worst mortality record of all social groups'. Their mortality rate was 42 per cent worse than the average rate for the Registrar General's lowest social class, class V, and 58 per cent of all the deaths in the group were attributed to 'external causes of injury'. They therefore report that there are more disadvantages for lone-parent children than those attributable to poverty (which itself is attributable to a significant degree to lone parenthood). Additional hazards are created for the child by being brought up in a situation where a family was never created by the marriage of the biological father to the mother, or where the family that had been created was broken by separation or divorce. Their conclusion is that 'class-based analyses which exclude them therefore produce a misleading picture of inequalities in child health'.[9] Judge and Benzeval studied economically-inactive lone mothers only. Children from father-absent families where the mother does go to work may find the problem of supervision exacerbated. As Ferri reported, lone parents 'who could literally not afford to take time off work often had to leave a sick child unattended'.[10]

'The children who experience conflict in two-parent families suffer just as much disadvantage as those who suffer conflict in one-parent families.' Again, that is broadly true. But the issue is not, do children experiencing the same degree of parental conflict, whatever their family situation may be, tend to show the same degree of disturbance, backwardness and deviance? The issue is, do children in one-parent families as a whole group tend to suffer more damage than children from two-parent families as a whole group? The universal answer is that they do, for the structural reason that the whole group of one-parent families is heavily weighted by those created by divorce, the result of conflicts that could not be resolved.

'Children who lack affection in the two-parent family show similar adverse traits to those who lack affection in the lone-parent family.' But that does not mean, as those who claim that 'the family is not deteriorating, only changing' argue, that there is no difference between two-parent and lone-parent families. For lone-parent families are structurally less efficient in producing flows of reliable, unconditional affection for their children than two-parent families. In good and successful lone-parent families this structural defect is compensated for by the special efforts of the mother and other people (and of course often is), or by the presence of other favourable factors as far as reliable, long-lasting and unconditional affection-giving is concerned.

In families of two successfully committed parents, if the supply of affection from one source is never present or temporarily or permanently dries up, there are on the average more alternative supplies than in the lone-parent family. This is technically bound to be so. Obviously in the worst case—the child who does not know who is father is, and in the extreme case even his mother does not—one complete set of potential givers of steady and unconditional affection are simply not available at all, namely, the father's relatives.

In any private arrangement of partners, with its greater tendency than the public institution of marriage to end up as a lone-parent arrangement, there is bound on average to be a deficiency of unconditionally committed affection. Long-term unconditional affection is not simply a matter of the love given by one or two people to their child. It is also a matter of the larger or smaller number of others potentially committed by kinship to supplying it.

What is the position of, for example, the grandfather? When it was a matter of shared cultural agreement, his role was characterized by the availability of his resource of *time*. The social demand (from which the practice of individual grandfathers deviated in some cases in exceeding the norm of what was socially required and in other cases dropping below it) was that this available time was drawn upon to attend to some tasks of simple supervision; in meeting the mother's wishes in other ways; and, with her express or implied consent or toleration, in indulging the grandchild to a degree greater than that which is either desirable or feasible for the parents. But, of incomparably the greatest importance to the child (and for the well-being of the grandfather) was the requirement of the unconditional affection that should suffuse all the otherwise rather arbitrary activities of this very limited role.

But it is one thing for him to be unconditionally attached to a grandson when the high chances of permanency of the relationship

65

is taken for granted by everybody. (In the normal case it will not be broken, but strengthened, by the death of either the grandchild's mother or father.) Every gesture, every look, can be set within the context of the relationship's development into the far future. But it is another matter entirely for the grandfather (as for all potential kinsfolk) if the relationship between the parents carries a much lower expectation of permanency. It is much more difficult for the grandfather to relate whole-heartedly—exactly the right word—to his grandchild when his access to the child is capable of being terminated or limited at any time.

Possibly these salient facts of the human condition are neglected because so few commentators who have dominated the mass media of communication during the past twenty years have themselves been grandparents. By making child-producing partnerships the private affair of two young adults, they have necessarily dissipated at the same time the cultural capital of grandparenthood from which their generation and previous generations had benefited. A society that has de-cultured marriage cannot hand on the best possible chance of four irrationally and permanently committed adults where the likelihood is relatively high that they will emotionally care, for as long as they live, about the children of their children, not so much for what they are, but for what they have meant to them as babies and infants. Indeed, without the grandparents of the old culture to mitigate the effects of the anomie of the new, it can be conjectured that the deleterious effects for children of the sexual revolution would have been addressed before the damage had become so widespread and the alteration in public opinion become so deep-seated.

Parents as partners instead of husbands and wives means that the whole system of kinship has been privatized, not just the marriage bond. The commitment of unconditional and irrational affection of kinsfolk cannot but be lessened when whether the parents stay together becomes a conditional decision, depending on what suits the partners in terms of the personal right of each to happiness and self-fulfilment.[11]

Not only does lone parenthood itself, therefore, necessarily mean a diminution in the number of potential givers of unconditional, long-term affection. The increase in the chances of partnerships and marriages ending as lone parenthood means commitment is more likely to be withheld across the board and from the start in all families of married couples and of all cohabiting partnerships, not just in lone-parent situations that already exist.

10

The Sea-Change In Public Opinion

There was a widely publicized case in mid-1993 of a child being disadvantaged by being brought up in a situation in which there was neither husband (the father had abandoned the mother), nor kinsfolk (the child's social-worker grandmother was not locally available), nor familiar neighbours (the mother and child were newcomers to the village of Lower Quinton, Warwickshire).

The mother earned about £500 a month with her uncle's firm in Stratford-upon-Avon. She paid £25 a week in rent; the rest was met by housing benefit. Child-minders were too expensive for her, so when the child was two years of age, she began to leave her alone all morning, driving home at lunchtime to see her. But her baby daughter would cling to her as she tried to return to work at 2 p.m. When the child was nearly three, the mother decided the child was old enough to be left alone for the whole nine hours she was away. She felt that returning home in the middle of the day, month after month, was 'an emotional burden'.

If the mother had depended on state benefits she would have lost £26.40 a week and the use of the company car; but she feared that she might assault her daughter if she gave up work and had to stay at home without her own means of transport in a strange village.

Germane Greer's response to this case was to draw attention to the fact that the father-absent family was now producing more children, while the father-present family was producing fewer. If there were going to be sufficient resources in the future from which old-age pensions could be paid, there would have to be a large enough population of working age to share the burden of providing them. Bearing a child who would in due course be a member of this population of working age was therefore 'as much as a public duty as the bearing of arms in the defence of the country', whether or not the child had a sociological father to bring it up. Were men the carriers of children there would have been no disguising what she calls this 'otherwise dubious fact'. Never-married lone mothers (along with other lone mothers) would then be 'housed, fed, paid, insured and trained for a profession of their choice', as soldiers are. We should not leave this never-married lone parent, therefore, to cope with the problems that remain for her within British society; we should welcome her, and provide for her as a 'professional career-mother'.

Greer's was a gloomy portrait of the mother in the father-absent household under present conditions. (She did not paint one of the father-absent child.) 'The mother on benefit, immobilized by her poverty, a virtual prisoner in her sub-standard accommodation, forced to communicate with nobody for hours, or days, on end, is a prime candidate for depressive illness.'[1]

There was nothing here to console the 'not deteriorating, only changing' school, beyond the argument that the appalling *faults* of the new father-absent arrangements were no greater than those where the father was present. But neither set of faults could possibly be remedied within the old framework of the cultural norms which prohibited conception and child rearing except by a permanently married man and woman. They could, however, be remedied by the state, and by creating a new culture in which no constraints of resources or disapproval would hinder a man or a woman from conceiving (or from risking conceiving) a child, whether or not there was a prior commitment by both of them to parenthood and spousehood.

Thus by the summer of 1993, under the pressure of the cumulative evidence from common experience and statistical studies, the weakness of the case that 'the family is not deteriorating, only changing' was increasingly exposed,[2] as was the discomfiture of its upholders when required to sustain it. The same thing seemed to be happening in the United States. A leading journal of liberal-left opinion published an article that caused something of a sensation. It did not simply break the media taboo on raising the question of whether one sexual and domestic life-style was better than another. It strongly argued that the evidence had now established beyond doubt the superiority, for the children and for the rest of society, of the family with two publicly and successfully committed natural parents. 'The social science evidence is in: though it may benefit the adults involved, the dissolution of intact two-parent families is harmful to large numbers of children. Moreover ... family diversity in the form of increasing numbers of single-parent and step-parent families does not strengthen the social fabric but, rather, dramatically weakens and undermines society'.[3] One of the major postulates of positive science is a version of the climber's dictum, 'If you try to beat the mountain, the mountain will beat you'. The facts can be ignored and denied, but they will relentlessly take their toll. There was a growing recognition that lone-parenthood was structurally and therefore necessarily inferior as a social device to the two-parent family.

Until 'fairly recently', Kathleen Kiernan writes, the 'prevailing wisdom' was that separation or divorce had few, and relatively small persistent effects on the lives of children.[4] But there was a growing recognition that the processes that created the lone-parent family by disruption had long-term and not just short-term consequences. Within the lone-parent category, she shows the usual relative advantage of children of widows. But the evidence she presents and, she writes, the evidence from other studies, suggests that marital breakdown has 'enduring' effects. On the notion that the diminution of stigma with the normalization of divorce might also diminish the effects of marital breakdown significantly, she says that on the evidence from the United States, we 'should not be too optimistic' about that.[5]

The average father-absent family is for the child's life chances inferior to the average family where the father had married the mother of their child before it was born. Orthodox social-affairs intellectuals who had for years denounced this as a scientific untruth and an obnoxious slander could now be heard protesting, 'No one has ever said that the lone-parent family is as effective as the two-parent family'.

People who had persevered in pointing that out now found themselves facing a number of new reactions. They were attacked not so much for what they said, but because of the way they said it. They should therefore say it in a way that upset no one. They were attacked on the grounds that the problems of the lone parent should not be exacerbated by publicizing the facts about them. They were attacked because what they said, though true, could be misused by those who had (to use Neil Kinnock's phrase) 'no intentions that could be described as good'. They should therefore say nothing. (The implications of the view that in a free society bad people could handle the truth but good people could not had not yet been adequately explored.) Given that for twenty years the very few publicizers of the facts had been constantly pilloried or lampooned; and that increasingly, from Agony Aunt to presenter of Woman's Hour, the basic wholesomeness of extra-marital sex and absent-father child rearing had been blandly propagated, the most bizarre charge from the media was that implied in the line of questioning, 'But haven't you chosen an easy target?', 'Do you think it is right to attack people who cannot answer back and put their case?'

The demagogic response of the spokespeople of the anti-family pressure groups was to confuse (perhaps because some of them were confused about) the appraisal of an individual case, on the one hand, and, on the other, the assessment of the efficacy of a specific system (or the anomic ineffectiveness of the state of affairs that succeeded it). To describe the system and its recent tendency towards entropy was, to these spokespeople, an attack on 'the single mum by moral authoritarians'. It was an attack, that is, on this Ms Brown and that ex-Mrs Smith—and on all of the other individual lone parents now in existence. This was the line taken even when, as with *Families Without Fatherhood*, the case that infuriated them was put by authors whose left-wing credentials were at least as good as theirs; when the whole of the emphasis of the work was not upon mums but upon men; and when the book was concerned throughout not with the success, the social-work aspect or the psycho-therapy of the individual case, but with the sociology of cultural change. It is just a fact of human nature that, unless we put some controls on our observations and feelings, you and I each of us know that in disputes we are in the right 99 per cent of the time. The difficulty of human relationships is that the person with whom you or I are in dispute knows with equal certainty that he or she is right 99 per cent of the time. These spokespeople could feel completely confident, therefore, that the real argument would be safely lost in a miasma of indignation and hurt feelings.

71

Yet the distinction is not difficult to make. It was made readily and clearly enough by the director-general of the British Association of Social Workers when he was called upon to clarify the position of a group of criticized social workers. The 'individual workers had acted reasonably', he said, but 'the structure had broken down'.[6]

The general reaction of all these former and continuing exponents of the 'not deteriorating' view, as well as some of those who had always admitted the facts of the inferiority of the lone-parent structure quā structure, was to say that, not only 'the clock could not be put back', but also that the momentum of change in the same direction was irresistible. The changes had already gone too far. They could not be stopped. They could not be decelerated. They certainly could not be reversed. All that could be done, then, was to provide ever-increasing public assistance to make up for the ever-growing shortfall in the resources formerly supplied by publicly and successfully committed married parents.[7] This argument proposed, that is, that because the people with the values and personal life-styles involved in unmarried parenthood (to take the easiest category) would not, could not and ought not to be expected to change, the people without their values and life-styles could and should be made to change in order to accommodate them.

Behaviour and values cannot be altered. Therefore the behaviour and values of the creators of unmarried lone-parent families cannot be altered. Why do the people who argue this way believe, then, that in order, say, to remove all stigma from the voluntary creators of unmarried lone parenthood, some married parents are able to change *their* conduct and values? Such people think it is important to discourage their own children from making choices they think will be detrimental to the welfare of their children and the welfare of their grandchildren. They think that the spread of the practice and the approval of cohabitation and father-absent families threatens their own welfare. Yet there is an expectation that *they* can change. Harriet Harman MP is a prominent Labour Party publicist. She is reported as having said, 'People go on about the importance of the family. It's so hurtful to single parents'.[8] These people are required, that is, not only to change by ceasing to disapprove of the father-absent situation and values. They are even required to change to the extent of ceasing to approve of their own situation and values.

To take another example: If unmarried lone-parent families are to enjoy more assistance, the behaviour and attitudes of the creators of stable two-parent families will have to be altered. They will have to improve their willingness to provide the resources that the lone parent and her or his children in general do lack, and once they are created do need. But, it is insisted, it is wrong to impose one's own values on other people, and therefore wrong to be judgemental about the voluntary creators of lone-parenthood. Where is the logic of the exponents of this view which allows them then to be judgemental about the stingy or evil people who are reluctant to increase the resources they supply to particular categories of lone parent?

As Weber said, when such questions are at issue it is not like being in a taxi with someone. You can stop a taxi wherever you like, and jump in or out of it just as it suits your purpose at the moment. It is like being in a tram car. You are in it together, and on the same lines, all the way to the next stop—Weber says all the way to the terminus. Put more bluntly, in these matters of altering conduct and of imposing one's values (or one's nihilism) on others, what is sauce for the married goose is sauce for the unmarried gander.

It may be that the multiplication of these problem-breeding arrangements for handling sexuality, child rearing and adult mutual aid will prove inexorable. But the weakening in what had been family *mores* may become widely recognized as a problem among the conforming intelligentsia, and not a preference or a matter of social indifference (which has been the case for the last twenty or thirty years). If and in so far as that happens, progress will be made in finding policies appropriate to discouraging some people from voluntarily creating lone-parent structures, while ameliorating the difficulties of their children who, without exception involuntarily, find themselves within them.

What is quite certain is that any policies aimed at strengthening the social institution of the family of two successfully committed parents that are not accompanied by, and embedded within, a profound change in the public opinion which the conforming intelligentsia has succeeded in creating, will fail. Without such a change in perception and attitude, at best the social policy-maker will continue to resemble Tawney's famous shoe-maker, who thought that the way to satisfy the customer who had complained of his shoddy workmanship was to make him a pair of equally shoddy shoes, but two sizes bigger; or today's equivalent of Tawney's church-goer, who thought she could make up for putting a counterfeit 50-pence piece in the collection one Sunday by putting in a counterfeit £1 coin the next.

Notes

Foreword

1 *The Times*, 2 October 1990.

2 *The Times*, 3 July 1991.

3 *The Times*, 20 September 1991.

4 *TLS*, 25 June 1993.

5 Melanie Phillips, 'The family and the left', *The Tablet*, 31 July 1993.

Chapter 1

1 Bogdanor, Vernon, and Skidelsky, Robert (eds.), *The Age of Affluence 1951-1964*, London: Macmillan, 1970.

2 The period of gradually rising crime in the 1940s and early 1950s was a period of rising standards of living. Rowntree and Lavers, in the study of York's poverty that has no place in the current social-policy canon, showed that on equivalent standards of 'poverty', 18 per cent of the working-class people of York were in their two poorest groups in 1936, and under 3 per cent in 1950. Rowntree, B. Seebohm, and Lavers, G.R., *Poverty and the Welfare State: A Third Social Survey of York Dealing Only with Economic Questions*, London: Longmans, 1951, pp. 30-31.

  Even now it is rare for a social commentator to deny the fact, when challenged, that *in absolute terms* it has improved beyond all recognition during the period of rising crime. The gap between dream of sufficiency for all reasonable purposes 70 years ago and the notion of poverty today cannot be better shown historically that through this quotation from the most influential book of one of the most influential intellectuals of the left during the pre-war period in this country, R.H. Tawney. 'The national output per head of population is estimated to have been approximately £40 in 1914. Unless mankind chooses to continue to sacrifice prosperity to the ambitions and terrors of nationalism, *it is possible that by the year 2000 it may have doubled.*' *The Acquisitive Society*, London: Bell, 1922, p.35. (Emphasis added.) He made this comment on the basis that the national output was already, in the early 1920s, adequate overall, and it merely had to be distributed more justly. Almost without exception critics have switched the argument to relative deprivation though, *suppressio veri, suggestio falsi*, some of them do not feel they have to be conscientious in removing the impression that things are absolutely worse.

3 As with weekly income, crime had been rising gradually, even though by present standards almost imperceptibly, at the same time as housing standards were rising between the wars.

The marked improvements in housing standards had formerly been documented and taken for granted as a fact even for the period covering the first half of the century. 'Between the Census of 1911 and the outbreak of war in 1939 some 5,000,000 new dwellings were built in Britain, *more than enough* to house the 3,350,000 additional families. But *even more striking* than this quantitative success was the improvement in the same period in the quality of the general level of housing conditions. ... Between 1921 and 1939 the proportion of the population living under conditions of gross overcrowding had been reduced by two-thirds, and the balance of the evil was by 1939 *small* and *highly localized* in the East end of London, and the cities of Tyneside and Scotland.' Abrams, Mark, *The Condition of the British People 1911-1945: A Study Prepared for The Fabian Society*, London: Gollancz, 1945, p. 44 and p. 49. (Emphasis added.) The improvements in the ratio of dwellings to people, internal space per person, and household amenities were far greater in the post-1945 period to date.

4 *Evening Chronicle* (Newcastle upon Tyne), 16 July 1993.

5 Home Office, *Criminal Statistics England and Wales 1938*, HMSO, 1939.

6 Figures compiled by Kemp Taylor and Stephen Anderson. *Echo* (Sunderland), 20 July 1993, pp. 1 and 5.

7 The rates are 'notifiable offences reported to the police, excluding other criminal damage valued at £20 or under, per 100,000 population per annum'. Home Office, *Criminal Statistics England and Wales 1991*, Cm 2134, London: HMSO, February 1993.

8 Stone, L., *The Family, Sex and Marriage in England 1500-1800*, London: Weidenfeld and Nicolson, 1977, pp. 38-39; Bromley, P.M., *Family Law*, 4th edn. London: Butterworth, 1971, p. 204; 5th edn., 1981, p. 187 n.3; Jackson, J., *The Formation and Annulment of Marriage*, 2nd edn., London: Butterworth, 1969, p. 39 n.3; *Report on One-Parent Families* (Finer Report), Cmnd 5629, London: HMSO, 1975, II, p. 92.

9 Dennis, G. (ed.), *Annual Abstract of Statistics 127*, London: HMSO, 1991.

10 *Ibid.*

11 Family Policy Studies Centre, *Family Policy Bulletin*, London: FPSC, December 1991.

12 Central Statistical Office, *Social Trends 23*, London: HMSO, 1993. The figures are for England and Wales.

13 Divorce in 1986 per 1000 existing marriages:

UK 13
Denmark 13
Netherlands 9
France 9
West Germany 8
Luxembourg 8
Belgium 7
Greece 3

Italy 1
Irish Republic 0

Social Trends 19, 1989, p. 45.
The figures were compiled by the Statistical Office of European Communities.

14 Haskey, J., and Kiernan, K., 'Cohabitation in Great Britain: Characteristics and Estimated Numbers of Cohabiting Partners', *Population Trends 58*, Winter 1989, p. 25.

15 Economic and Social Research Council, *ESRC Research Briefings No. 8*, London: ESRC, Autumn 1993.

16 In a study carried out by the Thomas Coram Trust, nearly half of the women cohabiting at the time of conception were lone parents by the time the child was aged 21 months. Nearly all the women who were married at the time of the conception of the child (16 out of 17) were not lone mothers. Phoenix, A., *Young Mothers?*, Cambridge: Polity Press, 1991.

17 In 1981 about one in three, but by 1991 about two in three births to teenagers were registered by both unmarried parents. But by 1991, also, about one-quarter of teenage births outside marriage were jointly registered by parents living at different addresses.

18 In the light of these low illegitimacy figures, a fact that has to be accounted for by those who allege that the man enjoyed pre- and extra-marital sexual intercourse just as frequently in the past as at the present, is that the cheap and reliable condom did not come into production until 1928, and that the contraceptive pill was not available until 1960.

The illegitimacy figures were kept low partly by 'shot-gun marriages', that is, the insistence by kin and neighbours that the man did take up his responsibilities. But they must have been kept low, too, by refraining to a far greater extent than is usual today from pre-marital intercourse. The prospect that if you 'got a girl into trouble' you were 'in trouble' yourself was a great dampener of sexual ardour.

It is occasionally proposed that the illegitimacy figures for earlier in this century are useless. They were kept low, it is said, by the fact that illegitimate children, in the numbers required to make up the difference between the figures then and the figures now, were not registered. Unless it is also proposed that infanticide was practised on a large scale, the difficulties in Britain of going about one's child's and one's own business for a number of years without a birth certificate seems to exclude this as a substantial explanation. To treat the infanticide hypothesis seriously for a moment: The proposition that large numbers of pregnant women in Great Britain in the twentieth century were able to dispose of their baby when it was born, without neighbours and the authorities requiring an adequate account of what had happened to it, is implausible. The *unmarried* pregnant woman was an especially conspicuous figure. It was not just a matter of disposing of a body. It was a body the existence of which in most cases had been obvious from the woman's pregnancy for many weeks. In this country at that time there was no question of infanticide

77

being tolerated either by the law or the *mores*, though of course associated with the general prohibition, and indeed as part of the system of *mores*, the near family members and perhaps some very few near neighbours would be expected to 'cover' for the poor mother if such a thing did occur. But it would in all circumstances be a very difficult thing to keep secret.

19 *Social Trends 21*, 1991.

20 *Social Trends 23*, 1993. Sue Slipman, of the National Council for One-Parent Families, asked more or less as a matter of course to comment in the ordinary intellectual press, or on radio or television when 'family matters' were an issue, easily fell into the imagery of the casual pick-up when talking about men and their relationship to their babies. 'Why should any woman in her right mind want to *take one home with her*?'—i.e. 'a man', who typically does not bring money or parenting skills into 'the relationships', and may be a vandal into the bargain. (*The Independent on Sunday*, 11 July 1993, p. 21, emphasis added.)

21 Haskey, J., 'Trends in the Numbers of One-Parent Families in Britain', in Office of Population Censuses and Surveys, *Population Trends 71*, London: HMSO, March 1993, p. 29.

22 Smith, Trevor, 'Influence of Socio-Economic Factors on Attaining Targets for Reducing Teenage Pregnancies', *British Medical Journal*, No. 6887, May 1993.

Both conception and birth among teenage women declined in the 1970s. They have risen steadily since 1983. This is dramatically different from the position in the societies which are often pointed to as the model for the future, the Scandinavian countries, where the legal restraints have been reduced, but where the force of social expectations has resulted in dramatic falls in teenage pregnancies and births. David, H.P., 'The United States and Denmark: Different Approaches to Health Care and Family Planning', *Studies in Family Planning*, 21, 1, 1990.

In this country in 1970 more than two-thirds of teenage pregnancies resulted in a birth within marriage. By 1980 abortion was the most common outcome. By 1990 it was a birth outside of marriage.

23 In *Families Without Fatherhood* George Erdos and I drew attention to the fact that a presenter of Woman's Hour, Jenni Murray, could now write with hardly an eyebrow being raised (least of all at the post-Reithian BBC) that marriage was an 'insult', that 'women should not touch it', and that she herself by becoming a wife had made herself into a 'legal prostitute'. (Murray, J., *Options*, July 1992, p. 8.) When we talk about Reith we have to remember, of course, that he has been discredited. He was an 'intolerant Scots moralist'. In public he was a man of stern values 'but [sic] his diaries show a man yearning for affection'. He is 'exposed' as a man who actually had a very close friend before he was married. When he first met him he wrote 'revealingly' in his diary that he was a 'very nice little chap. I like him'. The friendship remained very close until Reith married. As two young men they thought nothing of sleeping in the same bed together when necessary, and did not bother to put on bathing costumes when they went swimming in private. See McIntyre, Ian, *The Expense of Glory: A Life*

of John Reith, London: Harper Collins, 1993, and *The Sunday Times*, 22 August 1993, s.1, p. 1 and s. 2, pp. 1-2.

24 The main consequences are for the children without sociological fathers, and in the long term also for the men themselves and their fellow-citizens. But the fall-out is widespread. The interplay between relaxed sexual *mores*, Western wealth and improved mobility has resulted, according to Karen Hein of the Albert Einstein College of Medicine in New York, in male 'sex tourists' from Europe and the United States making 15- to 19-year-old women in places like Thailand the group with the highest incidence of HIV infection. Hein also reported that the HIV infection rate among 'US-American' women aged between 13 and 21 had risen by 77 per cent in the previous two years (of course from a low base); this group also had the highest incidence of venereal diseases such as syphilis and gonorrhoea. Michael Merson, Director of the World-Aids Programme of the WHO, said that the infection of female teenagers was largely due to infected men who did not use a condom. *Die Welt*, 21 July 1993, p. 12.

Why should sexually permissive men put the welfare of a purely sexual partner before their own purely sexual pleasure?

25 Dennis, Norman and Erdos, George, *Families Without Fatherhood*, London: IEA Health and Welfare Unit, 1992.

26 Least of all do I mean the awesomely narrow-minded and mechanical instruction in schools called sex education. For a critique, see Riches, Valerie, *Sex and Social Engineering*, Milton Keynes: Family and Youth Concern, 1986.

Chapter 2

1 Mills, C. Wright, The Cultural Apparatus' (1959), in Horowitz, Irving, L. (ed.), *Power, Politics and People: The Collected Essays of C. Wright Mills*, London: Oxford University Press, 1963, p. 405.

2 Weber, Max, *Economy and Society: An Outline of Interpretive Sociology*, Berkeley: University of California Press, 1978, p. 15.

3 Weber, Max, 'Science as a Vocation' (1919), in Gerth, H.H., and Mills, C. Wright (eds.), *From Max Weber: Essays in Sociology*, London: Routledge and Kegan Paul, 1948, p. 145. (Emphasis added.) The world-view of interpretative sociology is itself, of course, a potential and proper subject for interpretative sociology.

4 See, for example, Tennyson's 'Locksley Hall' (1842):

Men, my brothers, men the workers, ever reaping something new:
That which they have done but earnest of the things that they shall do:

For I dipt into the future, far as human eye could see,
Saw the Vision of the world, and all the wonders that would be;

Saw the heavens filled with commerce, argosies of magic sails,

Pilots of the purple twilight, dropping down with costly bales; ...

Till the war-drum throbb'd no longer, and the battle flags were furl'd
In the Parliament of man, the Federation of the world.

There the common sense of most shall hold a fretful realm in awe,
And the kindly earth shall slumber, lapt in universal law.

The Works of Alfred Lord Tennyson Poet Laureate, London: Macmillan, 1890, p. 101.

5   See, for example, Marx and Engels' celebrated sketch in *The German Ideology* (written 1845-46) of what a communist society would soon look like: 'Society regulates the general production and thus makes it possible for me to do one thing today and another tomorrow, to hunt in the morning, to fish in the afternoon, rear cattle in the evening, criticize after dinner, just as I have a mind ... ' (London: Lawrence and Wishart, 1970, p. 53.)

6   For example, Nietzsche, Friedrich, W., *Thus Spake Zarathustra* (1883-91), London: Dent, 1933; Sorel, Georges, *Reflections on Violence* (1908), London: Allen and Unwin, 1916. The phrase is Horowitz'. Horowitz, Irving Louis, *Radicalism and the Revolt Against Reason*, Carbondale, Ill.: Southern Illinois UP, 1968. Georg Lukács called one of his books 'the wrecking of rationality'. (*Die Zerstörung der Vernunft*, Darmstadt: Luchterhand, 1962.)

7   The spirit of nineteenth-century optimism about the application of science to social affairs—and its clear connection with enthusiasm for a united Europe under the control of expert commissioners—is beautifully caught by the title of one of Comte's most accessible works: Comte, Auguste, *A General View of Positivism: Or, Summary Exposition of the System of Thought and Life, Adapted to the Great Western Republic, Formed of the Five Advanced Nations, The French, Italian, Spanish, British, and German, Which, Since the Time of Charlemagne, Have Always Constituted a Political Whole* (1848), London: Trübner, 1865. This volume was a separately published version of the Introduction to Comte's *Treatise on Positive Polity*.

8   Stirner, Max [Schmidt, Johann Caspar], *The Ego and its Own* (1845), London: 1907. Stirner's meaning for 'das Einzige' is probably better conveyed by saying the egoist rather than the ego. Substantial sections of Marx' *The German Ideology* are taken up in mocking Stirner. With the dismantlement of the institutional control of sex and child rearing in the last twenty years, Stirner has come back to have the last laugh.

9   The phrase, of course, is that of the notorious radical, Paine. Paine, Thomas, *The Age of Reason: Being an Investigation into True and Fabulous Theology* (1794), New York: Willey Book Company, no date. My copy came to me from the Circulating Library of the Secretarial Training Department of the National Committee Y.M.C.A. of China—an interesting relic of the confidence that the West was the pattern for the rest of the world to imitate.

10 Arendt, Hannah, 'On Violence', *Crises of the Republic*, Harmondsworth: Penguin, 1973, p. 87.

11 Marx, Karl, 'Preface to *A Contribution to the Critique of Political Economy*', in *Selected Works*, Volume I, Moscow: Foreign Languages Publishing House, 1958, pp. 362-63.

12 These was the causes offered by the Archbishop of Canterbury for the arson and looting that occurred on North Tyneside and in Newcastle upon Tyne in September 1991.

A Church of England clergyman working full-time on the estate blamed material poverty for its problems. He had little time for the proposition that the residents bore some responsibility for their own condition. Declining to draw on the rich and ancient vocabulary of the Anglican tradition, when he was asked whether the Church of England bore any blame by having abdicated its responsibility for moral teaching, his answer was that that was 'crap'. He did concede that 'spiritual poverty' was an element in the estate's problems. *The Sunday Times*, 11 July 1993, p. 12.

13 Porter, Roy, 'Happy Families', *The Sunday Times*, 8 August 1993, s. 6, pp. 1-2.

14 Hegel, G.W.F., *The Philosophy of Right* (1821), London: 1896.

15 Comte, Auguste, *The Positive Philosophy* (1830-42), London: Trübner, 1853.

16 Hobhouse, L.T., *Morals in Evolution: A Study in Comparative Ethics*, London: Chapman and Hall, 1915.

17 This is W.I. Thomas' pregnant dictum. For a discussion of this point see Dennis, Norman, 'Sociology and the Spirit of Sixty-Eight', *British Journal Of Sociology*, 40, 3, September 1989, pp. 428-9.

18 See, for example, Parsons, Talcott, *The Structure of Social Action: A Study of Social Theory with Special Reference to a Group of Recent European Writers* (1937), London: Collier-Macmillan, 1968.

19 Durkheim, Emile, *The Division of Labour in Society* (1893), Glencoe, Ill.: Free Press, 1947, p. 32.

20 See Dennis and Erdos, 'What's Left and Right in Childrearing, Sex and Face-to-Face Mutual Aid?', *Families Without Fatherhood*, London: IEA Health and Welfare Unit, 1992, pp. 60-78.

21 Marx, Karl, and Engels, Frederick, 'The Communist Manifesto', *op. cit.*, pp. 36-37.

22 Schumpeter, J.A., *Capitalism, Socialism and Democracy*, London: Unwin, 1943, pp. 145-6.

23 *Ibid.*, p. 144.

Chapter 3

1 'An imaginary foreign observer' is not required for Orwell's case. This is exactly what did strike George Santayana about the Englishman (*Soloquies in England*): 'His character is like his climate, gentle and passing readily from dull to glorious,

and back again; variable on the surface, yet perpetually self-restored and invincibly the same'.

2 My attention was drawn to these striking quotations from Orwell and Gorer by Professor Christie Davies. See his 'Moralization and Demoralization: A Moral Explanation for Change in Crime, Disorder and Social Problems', in Anderson, Digby (ed.), *The Loss of Virtue: Moral Confusion and Social Disorder in Britain and America*, London: Social Affairs Unit, 1992, p. 6.

Orwell, George, 'The English People' (1944), in Orwell, Sonia, and Angus, Ian (eds.), *The Collected Essays, Journalism and Letters of George Orwell*, Vol. III, London: Secker and Warburg, 1968, pp. 2-3 and p. 8; Gorer, Geoffrey, *Exploring English Character*, London: Cresset, 1955, p. 16.

3 Smellie, K.B., *The British Way of Life*, London: Heinemann, 1955, pp.24-25. The passage quoted by Smellie may well be Gorer—it sounds like him—so it must not be doubled-counted in the evidence.

4 Hoggart, Richard, *The Uses of Literacy: Aspects of Working-Class Life with Special Reference to Publications and Entertainments*, Harmondsworth: Penguin, 1958, p. 137.

5 Carstairs, G.M., *This Island Now: The B.B.C. Reith Lectures 1962*, Harmondsworth: Penguin, 1964.

6 Dennis, Norman, and Halsey, A.H., *English Ethical Socialism*, Oxford: Oxford University Press, 1988.

7 Clutterbuck, Richard, *Britain in Agony: The Growth of Political Violence*, Harmondsworth: Penguin, 1980, p. 229.

8 *Die Welt*, 6 July 1993.

9 Local journalists are closer than their national counterparts to the 'toad beneath the harrow': the old woman mugged in a street long familiar to them; the arson attack on perhaps their old school; the known family whose windows are broken in revenge for mildly trying as good neighbours to control vandals. Award-winning writers like Frank Entwisle and Carol Roberton of the *Sunderland Echo* have eloquently, continually and from an early stage defended community and family values against the socially-rootless bureaucracies and the commercially-driven entertainment industry that have between them done so much to create the young men who have made the North East's Ragworths, Meadow Wells and West Ends increasingly the scene of domestic confusion and criminal intimidation.

Chapter 4

1 Cohen, Stanley, *Folk Devils and Moral Panics*, London: Macgibbon and Kee, 1972; Cohen, Stanley, and Young, Jock, *The Manufacture of News: Deviance, Social Problems and the Mass Media*, London: Constable, 1973; Cohen, Stanley (ed.), *Images of Deviance*, Harmondsworth: Penguin, 1976.

2　'Sociology and the Spirit of Sixty-Eight', *British Journal of Sociology*, 40, 3, September 1989.

3　Anson, Brian, 'Don't Shoot the Graffiti Man', *Architects' Journal*, 2 July 1986.

4　See, for example, Mailer, Norman, 'The White Negro: Superficial Reflections on the Hipster', first published in the summer 1957 edition of *Dissent*, and republished with a good deal of other interesting material on the same subject, in his *Advertisements for Myself*, New York: Signet Books, 1960, pp. 302-22.

5　Fanon, Frantz, *The Wretched of the Earth*, Harmondsworth: Penguin, 1967, reprinted 1969, p. 74.

6　'The *barbarous* exploits of famous bandits were celebrated by the peasants in a thousand songs and legends.' Ward, A.W., Prothero, G.W., and Leathes, Stanley, *The Cambridge Modern History*, Vol. X, The Restoration, Cambridge: Cambridge University Press, 1907, p. 173. Emphasis added—of course an intellectual in England in the early twentieth century was very unlikely to feel, and still less to show any solidarity with the bandit.

7　I mention only Stirner and Dostoyevsky in passing. The disparagement of the *ideals* of public morality (as distinct from criticism of those who hypocritically fall away from the ideal *in practice*) as all a fraud has won a ready response from intellectuals in all urban-industrial societies, though probably to a lesser extent until the 1960s in England than in the rest of Europe, and probably to a lesser extent in the United States to this day. The world of Balzac's hero, Vaudin, is built on this premise of the fraudulence of bourgeois culture in the nineteenth century. (Balzac's best known bon mot is probably 'Behind every fortune there is a crime'.) In this century the underworld of Brecht's *Threepenny Opera* is built upon the same premise.

　　What is new is that until the second half of the twentieth century these ideas did not reach a large section of the young through their experience in institutions of higher education (I am not referring by any means only what they are formally taught); and they did not reach large sections of the rest of the population through the media of popular entertainment and instruction.

8　In September 1993 a few dozen residents of Newcastle's crime-plagued West End, for all the world like characters out of some cowboy picture in the relatively inoffensive 1950s who had at last plucked up the courage to stand up to the bad guys, marched in fear and trepidation (as they admitted), but march they did, placards held high. They said they did not expect anything very practical to come of it, except perhaps having their windows smashed for their presumption. They simply wanted to show their *defiance* of the vigorous young men and boys who were constantly breaking into their homes, assaulting and robbing the old and weak, and defacing and destroying the amenities of their neighbourhood. (BBC 'Look North', 10 September 1993.)

9　Horkheimer, Max, and Adorno, Theodor, W., *Dialectic of Enlightenment*, London: Allen Lane, 1947, p. xii.

10　*Ibid.*, p. 4.

11 See Sheehan, Neil, Smith, Hedrick, Kenworthy, E.W., and Butterfield, Fox, *The Pentagon Papers*, New York: Bantam, 1971.

12 Arendt wrote that the 'new undeniable glorification of violence by the student movement' had this peculiarity: while the rhetoric of the new militants was clearly inspired by Fanon, they claimed to be Marxists. 'This is indeed quite baffling to anybody who has ever read Marx or Engels. Who could possibly call an ideology Marxist that has put its faith in "classless idlers", and believes that "in the lumpen-proletariat the rebellion will find its urban spearhead", and trusts that "gangsters will light the way for the people"?', *op. cit.*, p. 97.

13 Marcuse, Herbert, *One-Dimensional Man: Studies in the Ideology of Advanced Industrial Societies*, Boston: Beacon Press, 1964, pp. 256-7.

14 Taylor, Ian, Walton, Paul, and Young, Jock, *The New Criminology: For a Social Theory of Deviance*, London: Routledge and Kegan Paul, 1973; Wiles, Paul (ed.), *The Sociology of Crime and Delinquency in Britain: II The New Criminologies*, London: Martin Robertson, 1976.

15 Connerton, Paul (ed.), *Critical Sociology: Selected Readings*, Harmondsworth: Penguin, 1976.

16 For example, 'Kinder, die töten. Woher kommt die Gewalt?' (Children who kill. Where is the violence coming from?), *Der Spiegel*, 9, 1993, pp. 232-42; see esp. 'Nun ist die ganze Hoffnung weg' (Now there is no more hope), pp. 241-42.

Paradoxically, specifically the James Bulger type of case remained the last outpost of the 'growth of crime is an illusion' school of thought. This was because it was one of the few cases where the number of crimes had not risen significantly. Parental fears 'fly in the face of government statistics that show no appreciable rise in the number of child killings in the past 20 years'. (*The Sunday Times*, 1 August 1993, s.1, p. 1.)

But what if the discussion had been about traffic, where 'the rise in crime is an illusion' school of thought has played no role, and not about murder, where it has? Parents perceive the roads as having become more dangerous. Child road casualties have not significantly increased. If the argument in this context was that the perceptions of parents of increased danger 'flew in the face of the facts', because official figures showed no significant rise in child road injuries and deaths, it would have been immediately recognized for the *logical* error it is. Because it is in the context of crime, its illogicality passes unremarked.

The increased dangers created by the automobile industry by producing more cars, like the increased dangers created by the pornography industry by producing more child molesters, have been combatted by intensifying adult control over children's outdoor (though not their indoor) activities, and diminishing children's freedom to play unsupervised in their own neighbourhoods (though not in their own rooms).

Chapter 5

1 McGregor, O.R., Blom-Cooper, L., and Gibson, C., *Separated Spouses*, London: Duckworth, 1970.

2 Rheinstein, M., *Marriage Stability, Divorce and the Law*, Chicago: 1972, p. 272.

3 *Report of the Royal Commission on Marriage and Divorce* (Morton Report), Cmd. 9678, London: HMSO, 1956, para. 69, p. xiii.

4 Rowntree, Griselda, 'Some Aspects of Marriage Breakdown in Britain During the Last Thirty Years', *Population Studies*, 1964, pp. 150-51.

5 A Group Appointed by the Archbishop of Canterbury, *Putting Asunder: A Divorce Law for Contemporary Society*, London: SPCK, 1966

6 The law of the land already gave spousehood priority over parenthood as the function of marriage. In 1948 the House of Lords in *Baxter v. Baxter* had ruled that the *chief* aim of marriage was not the procreation of children; it was conjugal companionship.

This had the authority of no less a genius than John Milton, one of the first advocates of divorce, though on grounds that are far from modern. 'It is vain that anyone chatters about liberty in parliament and in the courts, if he is in servitude to an inferior at home—a kind of servitude most shameful to a man.' ('A Second Defence of the English People', in *The Portable Milton*, Harmondsworth: Penguin, 1976, p. 214.) Nevertheless, it was 'the solitariness of man' that God had ordered to prevent by marriage. 'A meet and happy conversation', he wrote, was its '*chiefest* and noblest end.'

In 1549 Thomas Cranmer had changed the Church of England liturgy to add 'mutual society, help, and comfort' to procreating children and remedying the sin of fornication as a cause for which God had ordained marriage. It had taken almost exactly four centuries for conjugal companionship to move from being for the first time one of the grounds for marriage to being the main one.

From *Baxter v. Baxter* it was a short and easy step in the course of the next four decades (in spite of abstract talk about 'the best interests of the child') for the conforming English intelligentsia to give, in their reaction to concrete cases, equality and then priority to the best interests of the parents, for example in the parents never marrying; in their divorcing; or in their working outside the home for self-fulfilment or extra money even when adequate child-care substitutes were no longer available from kinsfolk, and not yet available from the state.

7 *Op. cit.*, paras. 55, 65, 66, and 98.

8 Cmnd 3123, London: HMSO, 1966, para. 15.

9 *Ibid.*, para. 23.

10 Abrams, Mark, *The Condition of the British People 1911-45: A Study Prepared for the Fabian Society*, London: Gollancz, 1945, p. 40. On the stability of the English family in the first half of the twentieth century through all these vicissitudes, see Seccombe, Wally, *Weathering the Storm*, London: Verso, 1993.

11 Cole, G.D.H., *The Post-War Condition of Britain*, London: Routledge and Kegan Paul, 1956, pp. 18-19.

12 ' ... the passionate invective which Bernard Shaw was to direct against the marriage habits *of the middle and upper classes.*' (Emphasis added.) Smellie, K.B., *The British Way of Life*, London: Heinemann, 1955, p. 36.

The action for divorce of the Duke of Argyll in 1963 was one of the last occasions on which passionate invective was used by a public figure against the marriage habits of the upper classes, or of any social class. The Duke had shown photographs of his wife with another man 'indulging themselves in a gross form of sexual relationship' to a mixed party in New York, and 'seemed to think it was a joke'. In delivering his judgement the judge at the Court of Sessions, Lord Wheatley, remarked acidly, 'I do not commend his standard of tastes or his habits'.

As to the Duchess: 'There is enough in her own admissions to establish that by 1960 she was a completely promiscuous woman whose sexual appetite could only be satisfied by a number of men'. She seemed to think that adultery with a married man was not a serious breach of the moral code 'if the man was not happy with his wife'. She had indulged in 'disgusting sexual activities' in order to gratify 'a debased sexual appetite'. Lord Wheatley said that her attitude to the sanctity of marriage was 'what moderns would call enlightened'. In plain language, it could only be called 'wholly immoral'. (*The Times*, 9 May 1963, p. 9.)

When the Duchess died in 1993 the comments of the respectable media on this divorce case provided a valuable marker to the change in perception and evaluation in the thirty years that had elapsed since 1963. Pushing the changes back into some indefinite time before the 1960s, Margaret Duchess of Argyll was now perceived and judged as a 'victim' of 'generational chauvinism'. Lord Wheatley had applied in 1963 'a set of assumptions which had simply gone out of date' by then.

'By today's standards, *to her credit* was the fact that the Duke had filed for divorce in 1959.' This comment could only mean that it was to her credit that she did not commit additional acts of adultery until her husband had petitioned for divorce for previous ones. (*The Sunday Times*, 1 August 1993, pp. 1-2. Emphasis added.)

Chapter 6

1 Jowell, Roger, Witherspoon, Sharon, and Brook, Lindsay (eds.), *British Social Attitudes 1986*, Aldershot: Gower and Social and Community Planning, 1986.

2 Economic and Social Research Council, *ESRC Research Briefings No. 8*, London: ESRC, Autumn 1993.

3 Public accounts of wife-beating and sexual abuse of daughters suggests that such relationships were the exception rather than the rule. In the Thompson case, for example, it is clear that the scandal of the father's conduct was kept secret by the mother and two daughters not only by their wish not to be exposed to the normal world of working-class respectability as outlandish freaks, but also because the father threatened to kill them all with the shotgun he possessed if they said anything. Neither of these things is compatible with the normality of

physical abuse and incest. When his two daughters shot their father dead with his own gun, the detective who was called later described the murder as 'an execution, really', and the judge imposed, without any public outcry against it, a two-year suspended sentence. Artley, Alexandra, *Murder in the Heart: A True-Life Psychological Thriller*, London: Hamish Hamilton, 1993.

4 Marris, Peter, 'Review of *The Classic Slum*', *British Journal of Sociology*, 23, 1, March 1972.

5 Roberts, Robert, *The Classic Slum: Salford Life in the First Quarter of the Century* (1971), Harmondsworth: Penguin, 1973, p. 24.

6 *Ibid.*, pp.24-25.

7 *Ibid.*, p. 53.

8 Mearns, Andrew, *The Bitter Cry of Outcast London: An Enquiry into the Condition of the Abject Poor* (1883), in Keating, Peter (ed.), *Into Unknown England 1866-1913: Selections from the Social Explorers*, London: Fontana, 1976, p. 99.

9 Dennis, Norman, and Halsey, A.H., *English Ethical Socialism*, Oxford: Oxford University Press, 1988.

10 See Millard, John, *Ralph Hedley: Tyneside Painter*, Newcastle upon Tyne: Tyne and Wear Museums, 1990, between pages 54 and 55. The popularity of the print dates from 1890, when it was published by the *Evening Chronicle* (Newcastle upon Tyne) as a Christmas souvenir.

11 This was originally published in *Allan's Tyneside Songs*, 1891, and is still included today in popular editions of nineteenth and early twentieth century working-class songs of the Wear and Tyne, e.g. in the *Geordie Song Book*, Newcastle upon Tyne: Graham, 1986, pp. 21-23.

12 Lawson, Jack, 'A Naked Philosopher', *A Man's Life*, London: Hodder and Stoughton, 1932.

13 *Ibid.*, pp. 63-64. I do not know how many copies were sold, but it was printed in August 1932, and was reprinted the next month, and again in September 1933.

In Lawson's day the life of the miner's wife in Boldon Colliery was hard. But given the conditions under which the family had to live, was the division of labour between husband and wife so very unfair? Current left-wing opinion, that the miner kept his wife slaving at housework, child-rearing, washing and shopping to 'service' him, while he selfishly kept the dust, the sweat, the darkness, the frustration, the anger, the danger, and the subordinate position of working nearly always to other people's instructions, all to himself, would have struck people in the pit villages of Co. Durham as scarcely capable of being held by sane people.

An anecdote so despised by the 'crime is an illusion' school of thought: an off-shore oil-rig worker, Keith Black, had just returned from a three-year world cycling tour that had taken him across Japan, Taiwan, Indonesia and New Zealand, and more recently from a cycling trip to Iceland. He parked and locked his bicycle in the entrance to the Asda supermarket in Boldon Colliery. When he

came out of the shop he found that it had been stolen. *Echo* (Sunderland), 20 July 1993, p. 8.

14 Humphrey, Robin, 'Life Stories and Social Careers: Ageing and Social Life in and Ex-Mining Town', *Sociology*, 27, 1993.

On 16 July 1993 Radio Newcastle featured a Ferryhill garage-owner, Norman Forster, who was electrifying its internal doors to administer a shock to intruders because, he alleged, he had been burgled 300 times (most probably on most occasions by young male Ferryhillers).

15 'Good sense is, of all things among men, the most equally distributed; for every one thinks himself so abundantly provided with it, that even those who are most difficult to satisfy in everything else, do not usually desire a larger measure of this quality than they already possess.' That may sound as though he had his tongue in his cheek; but he continues, 'And in this it is not likely that they are all mistaken; the conviction is rather to be held as testifying that the power of judging aright and of distinguishing truth from error, which is properly called good sense or reason, is by nature equal in all men'. Descartes, René, *Discourse on Method* (1637), London: Dent, 1912, p. 3.

16 *Ibid.*

17 For an discussion of the differences in knowledge conveyed by the mass media of communication and that discussed in small circles of the public all of whom has direct knowledge of the affair, the distinction between what he calls 'mass society' and 'communities of publics', see Mills, C. Wright, 'Mass Society and Liberal Education'(1954), in Horowitz, Irving, L. (ed.), *Power, Politics and People: The Collected Essays of C. Wright Mills*, London: Oxford University Press, 1963, pp. 353-73.

18 See Dennis, Norman, *People and Planning: The Sociology of Housing in Sunderland*, London: Faber and Faber, 1970; *Public Participation and Planners' Blight*, London: Faber and Faber, 1972.

19 Cobbett, William, *Rural Rides* (1821-1832), Vol. II, London: Dent, 1912, p. 31.

20 'Labour Stakes Claim to be Party of Community Care', *The Independent*, 21 September 1990.

Chapter 7

1 Dean, Malcolm, 'No Case for Hiding in the Bunker', *The Guardian*, 27 February 1993. Dean, a Guardian reporter, recognizes that he is part of the conforming consensus on the family, and includes his readers in it. 'So Guardian man (and Guardian woman) should hang their heads in shame today ... it is time to brood guiltily over Chelly Halsey's philippic against liberals and the left for torpedoing the traditional two-parent nuclear family ... Where have we heard all this before? ... from Margaret Thatcher.

2 *The Guardian*, 23 February 1993.

3   Ferri, Elsa, 'Background and Behaviour of Children in One-Parent Families', *Therapeutic Education*, 3, 2, 1975.

The NCDS showed that the children from two-parent families whose average life chances were best were not the legitimate children from the home of their two natural parents. The children who do best were those with two adoptive parents.

Those whose average life chances were worst were the illegitimate children who were brought up by both the parents who were the cause of their illegitimate birth. In this group the 'illegitimate father' was a handicap to the child. The life chances of the illegitimate child were improved somewhat on average when the illegitimate father was not part of the household.

4   The largest group—54 per cent—were those whose parents had experienced marital breakdown, the next largest group—35 per cent—were those whose mothers were widows.

5   *Op.cit.*

6   *Ibid.*

7   *Ibid.* (Emphasis added.)

8   *Ibid.* See also Ferri, E., 'Growing Up in a One-Parent Family', *Concern*, 20, 1976; Ferri, E., 'One-Parent Families', *Journal of the Association of Workers for Maladjusted Children*, 4, 1, 1976; Ferri, Elsa, and Robinson, Hilary, *Coping Alone*, Windsor: NFER, 1976; Ferri, E., 'Children in One-Parent Families', *Ginger*, February 1979.

9   Ferri, Elsa, *Growing Up in a One-Parent Family: A Long-Term Study of Child Development*, Windsor: NFER, 1976, Table A12.12.

10 'The reading scores of illegitimate children whose mothers had worked full-time [in the previous year] did not differ significantly from those of children in other family situations from non-manual backgrounds. They were, however, significantly better in reading than those of children from *manual* backgrounds who were living with both parents or with divorced or separated mothers.' *Ibid.*, Table A12.8, p. 111. It is not clear from the text whether the number is 25 or 26.

11 Social class background of illegitimate children being brought up at age 11 by mother alone:

Social class	percentage	No.
1	0.0	0
2	2.5	1
3 non-manual	12.5	5
3 manual	42.5	17
4	22.5	9
5	20.0	8
	100.0	40
No information		18
Total		**58**

12 Economic and Social Research Council, *ESRC Research Briefings No. 8*, London: ESRC, Autumn 1993. (Emphasis added.)

13 *The Works of Edmund Burke*, Vol. IV, London: Oxford University Press, p. 285.

14 Ezek. 18. 2. Cf. Lam. 5. 7.: 'Our fathers have sinned, and are not; and we have borne their iniquities'.

Chapter 8

1 James, Oliver, 'Vicious Outcome of the Poverty Trap', *The Observer*, 23 May 1993.

2 Crellin, E., Kellmer Pringle, M.L., and West, P., *Born Illegitimate: Social and Economic Implications*, Windsor: NFER, 1971, p. 90.

3 'Cases' means here 'life-chance areas'. Of course there were 'cases' of some individual children in the category doing better than some individual legitimate children from two-parent families—a point we are constantly making, but a point that constantly for the past twenty years the media have innocently misinterpreted or wilfully obfuscated.

4 *Ibid.*, p. 109.

5 Phillips, Melanie, 'The Family and the Left', *The Tablet*, 247, 7982, 31 July 1993, p. 972. (Emphasis added.) She presented this account as one of three small indicators of the intellectual climate surrounding these issues.

The second indicator was the fact that, after writing an article in the *Observer* in favour of settled family life, she was 'furiously taken to task by an academic historian of liberal views' who said that 'he for one did not believe any of this so-called evidence that fragmented family life did children harm'.

The third indicator was that at a Fabian seminar on family values held at Christmas 1992, a platform speaker said ('not without some trepidation') that generally a child's best interests were served by being brought up by its own mother and father. He was complimented from the floor for expressing an opinion that 'could not now be voiced without a great deal of courage'.

6 Riley, David, and Shaw, Margaret, *Parental Supervision and Juvenile Delinquency*, Home Office Research Study No. 83, London: HMSO, 1985.

7 *Ibid.*, p. 34, p.44.

8 Riley says that his chapter 6 includes a detailed discussion of the relationship between delinquency and family characteristics in one-parent households. It does not include a 'detailed' discussion at all.

9 Lambert, Angela, 'Don't Throw Stones At Us', *The Independent*, 12 July 1993. (Emphasis in original, paragraphing added for clarity.)

10 Dickens, Charles, *Oliver Twist* (1838), Ware, Herts.: Wordsworth, 1992, p. 483.

Chapter 9

1 Bradshaw, J., and Millar, J., *Lone-Parent Families in the UK*, London: HMSO, 1991.

2 Furstenberg, F., *Adolescent Mothers in Later Life*, Cambridge: Cambridge University Press, 1987; Kamerman, S., and Kahn, A.J., *Mothers Alone: Strategies for a Time of Change*, Dover, Mass.: Auburn House, 1988.

3 *Op. cit.*, p. 64.

4 *Ibid.*, pp.20-21

5 *Ibid.*, p. 21. This refers to 'equivalent net disposable resources'.

6 Burghes, Louie, *One-Parent Families: Policy Options for the 1990s*, York: Joseph Rowntree Foundation, February 1993.

7 Hudson, F., and Ineichen, B., *Taking It Lying Down: Sexuality and Teenage Motherhood*, London: Macmillan, 1991, pp. 203-07; Phoenix, A., *Young Mothers*, Cambridge: Polity Press, 1991, pp. 151-59.

8 Office of Population Censuses and Surveys, *Mortality Statistics Perinatal and Infant: Social and Biological Factors 23*, London: HMSO, 1992; *Congenital Malformations 1990*, 1992.

9 Judge, Ken, and Benzeval, Michaela, 'Health Inequalities: New Concerns About the Children of Single Mothers', *British Medical Journal*, 306, 13 March 1993, p. 677. Those father-absent children who were in the age group 10-15 were over four times more at risk of dying than all children from RG classes I and II.

10 Ferri, Elsa, 'Background and Behaviour of Children in One-Parent Families', *Therapeutic Education*, 3, 2, 1975.

11 There is a profound difference between the *individual desire* to have a baby along with a 'loving relationship', and the *social requirement* that if there is to be a child, it must have an effective sociological father and an effective mother for many years of its life, whether or not the relationship between the consenting couple ends up by being a 'loving' one. This does not always seem to be fully appreciated. 'I have never met a single parent who would not give her eye teeth for a loving relationship with a man.' (Sue Slipman, National Council for One-Parent Families, *The Independent on Sunday*, 11 July 1993, p. 21.) 'Young people aren't given much support to make responsible decisions ... of what it is like to go out with someone and discuss whether they are ready for sex.' (Karin Pappenheim, Family Planning Association, *ibid.*)

Chapter 10

1 Greer, Germane, 'The Hard Facts of Motherhood: It Is Time Mothers Were Given More Help and Less Blame', *The Sunday Times*, 8 August 1993, s. 1, p. 9.

2   See, for example, *The Sunday Times*, 11 July 1993; *The Independent on Sunday*, 11 July 1993, p. 21.

  The Independent on Sunday was particularly interesting because it featured more of the representatives of the conventional consensus than did The Sunday Times, and was marked by the considerable modification in the positions they had hitherto adopted. Its feature was actually entitled 'Absent Fathers'. Sue Slipman (National Council for One-Parent Families), remained more firmly attached to her former position than other commentators: Women have been claiming rights of their own, 'rather than existing as the property of men inside marriage'. The real reason that the government will not supply 'a little investment' to allow lone mothers to go out to work, she is reported as saying, is that it 'is horrified by the fear' (sic) that women could 'get by without men' *and* 'be independent of the state'.

3   Whitehead, Barbara Dafoe, 'Dan Quayle Was Right', *The Atlantic Monthly*, April 1993.

4   Kiernan, Kathleen. E., 'Impact of Family Disruption on Transitions Made in Young Adult Life', *Population Studies*, 46, 1992, p. 213.

5   *Ibid.*, pp. 233-24.

6   Ellis, Walter, 'Clueless, Tactless or Hapless: What is a Social Worker?', *The Sunday Times*, 18 July 1993.

7   'Mr. [David] Utting commented that *he could see no point* in stressing the link between crime and single parenthood because to do so was futile. "Are you going to outlaw divorce?", he asked.' Janet Daley, 'Should We Ignore the Link between Crime and Broken Homes Because We Feel Helpless About It?', *The Times*, 1 July 1993. (Emphasis in original.) 'I do not think we have very much choice but to accept the new shape of families', Patricia Hewitt, deputy director of the Institute of Public Policy Research, *The Independent on Sunday*, 11 July 1993.

8   *The Sunday Times*, 11 July 1993, p. 14.

From the IEA Health & Welfare Unit

The Spirit of Democratic Capitalism
Michael Novak, £7.95, 463pp, February 1991

Novak...has done us a service in illuminating where the fault lines between right and left now lie.

> Will Hutton, The Guardian

Mr Major...might seek inspiration from The Spirit of Democratic Capitalism by Michael Novak.

> Joe Rogaly, Financial Times

God and the Marketplace
Jon Davies (editor), £4.90, 145pp, 1993

[The IEA's booklets] have the merit of seeking to debate the morality of wealth creation.

> Joe Rogaly, Financial Times

various Christian theologians welcome the economic role of the market and endorse wealth creation as a primary good.

> Daily Telegraph

The Family: Is it just another lifestyle choice?
Jon Davies (editor), £6.95, 120pp, 1993

The report says that society is paying a heavy price for the belief that the family is just another lifestyle choice.

> The Times

The Moral Foundations of Market Institutions
John Gray, £7.95, 142pp, February 1992

This powerful tract ... is persuasive.

> Andrew Adonis, Financial Times

one of the most intelligent and sophisticated contributions to conservative philosophy.

> Roger Scruton, The Times

Also From the IEA Health & Welfare Unit

Working Class Patients and the Medical Establishment
David Green, £9.95, 211pp, 1985

a unique study of the development of the relationship between producers and consumers ...in the hundred years up to the creation of the National Health Service.

Political Quarterly

an important if controversial contribution.

Sociology

Equal Opportunities: A Feminist Fallacy
Caroline Quest et. al., £6.95, 111pp, 1992

The authors argue that all equality legislation should be abolished so that the free market can operate without any restraint.

The Independent

Laws banning sex discrimination and promoting equal pay at work damage the intersts of women the Institute of Economic Affairs claims today.

Daily Telegraph

Let us not above all be politically correct. Let us not become overheated because the Institute of Economic Affairs has brought out a startling report entitled *Equal Opportunities: A Feminist Fallacy.*

The Times

Laws which effectively promote "preferential hiring" policies "harm women" according to an essay in a recent book from the Institute of Economic Affairs.

Industrial Relations Review and Report

Subscription Service

The easiest way to obtain IEA Health and Welfare Unit publications is to take out a subscription. The cost is only £9.00 per year, or £15.00 for two years.